Motherhood

Motherhood

AN EXTRAORDINARY VOCATION

DR. KATHRYN ROMBS

Our Sunday Visitor
Huntington, Indiana

Our Sunday Visitor Publishing Division
Our Sunday Visitor, Inc.
200 Noll Plaza
Huntington, IN 46750
1-800-348-2440

ISBN: 978-1-68192-680-3 (Inventory No. T2552)
1. RELIGION—Christian Living—Calling & Vocation.
2. RELIGION—Christian Living—Calling & Vocation.
3. RELIGION—Christianity—Catholic.

eISBN: 978-1-68192-681-0
LCCN: 2021930119

Cover and interior design: Chelsea Alt
Cover art: Anna Mein
Interior art: Bridgeman Images; Pixabay; Public domain/Wikimedia Commons

PRINTED IN THE UNITED STATES OF AMERICA

*To Patricia Phillippi, who inspired me
by her extraordinary example to give
my life to Catholic motherhood*

TABLE OF CONTENTS

INTRODUCTION
AN ADVANCE FOR
MOTHERHOOD

To me, as a teenager growing up on the Upper East Side of Manhattan, little children seemed burdensome — their awkward strollers tumbling over uneven pavement, their nannies taking them to playgrounds in Central Park, their little mittens dropping in the black puddles of polluted, melted snow. Whether I was walking down Fifth Avenue past the Metropolitan Museum of Art or scurrying down the Eighty-Sixth Street subway stairs, I saw parents hurrying children along or keeping them from getting hit by a city bus. Every once in a while, I saw mothers or fathers who seemed enraptured with their children. But much more often, these accomplished, refined adults were taking a break from their important lives to talk to their children with wide eyes and stilted voices. Sometimes I got the impression that these parents were just on pause until they got back to their real lives, their main interests, and their professional ambitions.

Why would I want to be a mother? I thought. *A child would take away from my productivity, from my chance to do something meaningful. A child would create too many interruptions as I pursue what I really want to do.* I attended an elite, Catholic private school in Manhattan. The doors were wide open for me to walk into the most sophisticated and worthy life callings. A senator? An executive? I could try to end world hunger. I could help rescue whole populations from poverty or illiteracy. Whether I went to Wall Street or the Third World, I was compelled to do something radical, something large-scale, something that history would remember. My descendants would have me to look up to, showing them a path to a fruitful, meaningful life. Scarcely could I have imagined the form my large-scale, high-impact vocation would take: the private life of motherhood.

My mother is a Christian feminist and is enrolled in the Woman's Hall of Fame. She is friends with Gloria Steinem, the famous feminist of the 1970s, and when I was growing up, they worked together on various projects, especially for low-income women and girls. I am grateful to my mother, who always wanted me to have the opportunity to pursue any career to which I felt drawn. I am thankful that she raised me to make a difference, both for the common good as well as for women in particular.

At age sixteen, I attended a meeting at Gloria Steinem's apartment in Manhattan. Gloria had invited my mom and me, along with a few other feminists and their daughters, to her home for a discussion on the theme of "Passing the Torch." Still wearing my private-school uniform and saddle oxfords, I sat in an upholstered armchair, munching cookies with white icing while listening to Gloria's message: It was time for teenage girls to take up the cause of feminism:

> Do not sit by passively and let others defend your rights. Don't you know that your generation might lose what we have gained for you? You, too, must fight for equal pay for equal work, for women to have a seat at the top of the corporate ladder, and for the world to expect females in public office. If you do not fight, we will lose ground. Your daughters and granddaughters are depending on you. So are we.

During my high school years, I showed all the signs of having a successful professional life ahead of me. Educated at the same school as the future Lady Gaga and Nicky Hilton, I served on the student council, led organizations, and made excellent grades. Upon graduation, I earned a handful of awards at the closing ceremonies.

But my interior life was a constant struggle. I had not yet learned that friendship is worth guarding, or that happiness comes through intangibles such as kindness, compassion, humility, and relationships with God, family, and loved ones. My Upper East Side lifestyle was blingy — Robert Redford lived on the floor above me, and Paul Newman lived in the building next door. But inwardly, my school years were fraught with pain. Between the ages of twelve and sixteen, I brushed up against drug experimentation and Lower Manhattan nightclubs. All the dating I did was impersonal and shallow. Many of the young women at my school were on birth control. The idea of getting pregnant was every girl's nightmare. With all the freedom most young people crave, a pocket full of cash, and no curfew, I was empty. My life was outwardly attractive, but felt to me like a wasteland of broken friendships and a broken heart.

In my late teens, with my mother's friendship and support, I became a Christian and traded my secular lifestyle for daily Bible reading and lots of quiet time to let God restore my soul. My mother cared deeply about my faith life. She helped me find churches and faith communities. During my last two years of high school, I chose the Bible, the photography darkroom, and the jogging trails in Central Park as my sacred grounds. I spent most of my after-school hours alone, developing black-and-white photographs, praying, and listening to the gentle voice of God. By the time I went to a university in North Carolina, I was a Christian with no clear creed and a feminist who was no longer at home with most feminists.

During college, I became interested in the Catholic Faith. In what seems now to me an amazing twist of fate, the Baptist group on campus to which I belonged led a retreat at Gethsemani, the Trappist monastery in Kentucky where Thomas Merton had been a monk. There I fell in love with monastic life and learned new ways to pray — *lectio divina*, contemplative prayer, and the Liturgy of the Hours. These became new ways to relate to God, satisfying a hunger for intimacy with him that my previous ways of praying, mainly vocal prayer, did not. I also cherished the times when I would steal away and pray by myself in the Catholic chapel on campus. I loved sitting in front of the tabernacle and feeling Christ's grace wash over me.

The next summer, inspired by my time in Gethsemani, I went on a retreat to an ecumenical monastery in France, but it was not the place for me, and I left within just a few hours. I soon found another retreat destination in France that happened to be Catholic, Saint Margaret Mary Alacoque's Convent of the Sacred Heart in Paray-le-Monial. I spent countless hours in adoration and fell in love with the Eucharist. It was in Mass there that I first felt the words bubble up in my heart: I need to become Catholic.

After college and a year living in a convent in Rome, I went to graduate school to study philosophy. My love for the Catholic Faith had continued to grow. My first Easter there, I was received into full communion with the Catholic Church. A year later, I fell in love with a faithful Catholic man who was getting his Ph.D. in early Christian theology. I was interested in the philosophy of religion and discovered the extraordinary thought of Saint Thomas Aquinas, on whom I wrote my dissertation. Ron and I got married while we were finishing our degrees. I was on my way to a fulfilling Christian family life.

As I was nearing the finish line for my Ph.D., I became pregnant with our son, Jacob. Ironically, I delivered him on the day I finished my dissertation. My 267-page document was flying to New York while I gave birth to our child in Washington, DC. I was overjoyed to be a mother. I experienced the most complete satisfaction and fulfillment I had ever felt, carrying this child first in my womb and then in my arms. I gave my days to holding and caring for this tiny, adorable creature. Awake in the nights, frazzled in the days, I gave everything to this newborn child. Not so often did I pore over books and articles. Not so frequently did I make regular treks to the library.

Now I spent most of my time on my baby, taking regular treks instead to the pediatrician and to the drugstore for diapers and pacifiers.

As fulfilling as it was to be a wife and mother, I wondered, "What is my calling?" I was still a person groomed for big accomplishments and high productivity. I had an outstanding education and lots of marketable skills. As much as I loved and cherished my husband and baby boy, I could not help but think: I am slipping backward. I am stuck. I am relegated to such menial tasks as dishes and laundry. I am on a survival mode, and some days I do not even feel as if I am surviving. I think I have lost any potential I might have had for doing something great with my life.

Then, slowly, over the next few years, I discovered my way. As I read the Scriptures and the works of Pope Saint John Paul II, and as I pondered the lives of many women in the history of Christianity, the eyes of my mind and my heart opened. Like walking through the wardrobe into Narnia, I discovered an unbelievable, incredible world I had not known existed: the extraordinary vocation of motherhood.

Christianity has always had a high regard for mothers, viewing motherhood as a gift from God, and heralding mothers in both the Old and New Testaments as chosen instruments in God's sovereign plan. The Catholic Church is a leader of our world in upholding the greatness of motherhood. She identifies a mother, Mary, as the archetype of humanity in its response to God, and the model for all human beings, both men and women, in their love for Christ. Christians recognize that motherhood has eternal significance. Whether we are biological or adoptive mothers, stepmothers or spiritual mothers, foster mothers or grandmothers, mothers of all kinds participate in the creation and rearing of beings made for union with God.

But motherhood has suffered. For millennia, the New Testament message of the dignity of women and the importance of the maternal vocation has been largely diminished, undervalued, and suppressed. Many women have been demeaned as second-class citizens. Many mothers have been taken for granted and mistreated.

Thus, in my view, there was something right about the feminists of the late nineteenth and early twentieth centuries, many of them Christians and mothers, taking the stance that "Women should have the right to vote." Then there was something right about the feminists of the sixties and seventies — even though many of them were not of the Christian tradition — saying, "Women should have the right to equal pay for equal work and should not be denied a job just because of their gender." They were right also in coining the term *domestic violence* so that, for the first time in history, women could protest being battered or beaten by their husbands.

But one thing many of the feminists of the 1970s got wrong was that they *left behind motherhood*. Feminists such as Gloria Steinem, Betty Friedan, and Bella Abzug were so focused on fighting for our right to education, our right to employment, and our right to public office — and I earnestly thank them for their achievements — that motherhood took a back seat. Motherhood was naturally seen as a hindrance to the opportunities that suddenly had been won for women; in the words of Gloria Steinem, "As long as females are valued only for our wombs, we will never be valued for our minds and hearts."[1]

For the past sixty years, many women in the West have advanced in all areas of the public sector. Thankfully, women's gifts and talents are making their imprint on our economy and businesses, medicine and health, the sciences, government, law, technology, education, literature, and the arts. And yet many of these women see motherhood as something that will detract from their professional development. They view motherhood as something that will hold them back, as a threat to their greatest success. They perceive it as resistance to their movement forward.

Alternatively, another strand of women in the West have resisted the pressure of professional pursuit and maintained marriage and motherhood as their main focus. Some young women have been accused of going to college to get their "Mrs. degree." But once many of these women are married with children, they answer the question, "What do you do?" with "I'm *just* a mother." How strange — that someone for whom motherhood is an ideal way of life still openly diminishes it. The age in which we live is marked by women either viewing motherhood as a threat to achieving something really great, or choosing motherhood as first in their lives, but adopting a vocabulary that relegates it as a distant second. Ours is not a culture that publicly appreciates motherhood.

It is time for that to change. It is time for the seed that was planted by Christ — the message of the dignity of motherhood — to bloom. It is time for women's advancement and the correction of history's wrong attempts to blot out femininity. These attempts obfuscate one of the central beauties and strengths of women: their ability to participate in God's creation and the formation of human beings. Mothers have the important job of rearing young people to enter the matrix of society, prepared to bring creativity, thoughtfulness, ingenuity, skill, and courage to make the world a better place. It is time for women — especially Christian women, and Catholic women in particular, since appreciating motherhood is the fulfillment of their Church's doctrine — to bring this change about themselves. It is time for mothers to take their places as leaders of our society, intently pursuing their professional lives if they so choose, while embracing motherhood and being "card-carrying mothers."

ℬ

The purpose of this book is to make the case that motherhood can be a significant part of the successful life of a twenty-first-century woman. Many women today, including faithful Catholic women, are ambivalent about motherhood. They see it as unimportant, suited for the unambitious; some women see it as compromising their careers, their personal development, and their happiness. If you have similar concerns, this book will help you sort out why motherhood is worth your time and best attention. It will lovingly validate your varied priorities, each of which has its own reasonability. Without providing a pat answer about work outside the home — since there are many good options and what is right for one woman is not right for all women — these pages will help you see what is so special about motherhood and recognize it as a vocation that can bring about your greatest fulfillment. In the end, whatever you decide regarding work outside the home, this book will help to make more meaningful each moment you are with your child or children.

ℬ

Do you ever worry about compromises you might have to make in your personal or professional life? Do you think you might not achieve your goals as fast as you would without having to chase little feet around your home? While many women crave having children, many women also desire financial security and professional success. These are precious assets that are rightly appreciated. How do you plan to balance family and career? Do you plan to work full-time? Or do you want to stay home as you raise your family? Or can you not yet imagine how your life will unfold, even what you hope for?

Twenty-two years into my marriage, I am a mother of six, and I teach philosophy — some semesters but not others — at the University of Dallas. Not only do I have many friends who wrestle with these questions, but I have gotten to know many students who come from a vast array of backgrounds. As I have spoken with many young women outside of class over the years, one thing I have noticed is that among college-educated women of all ages, the question of how family life will interface with professional life is a major topic of interest.

Some of these young women want to work because their careers are genuinely important to them. Others want advanced degrees and the chance for a professional life, but they want to stay home with young children. Still others hope to remain home full-time. Careers are important to women today, and so is family. Even women who have raised their children revisit these questions as they have more time on their hands, and begin looking for new avenues of personal fulfillment and opportunities to strengthen their financial situations. There is a range of preferences for how to balance career and family. There is no right or wrong regarding full-time work, and it is important that women support each other in their different choices. Each woman has to find what is right for her in the various seasons of her life.

It is time for a new era, one in which women are appreciated both for what they can contribute to the public sector, and also for their vocation as mothers. The goal is a new kind of motherhood: aware of its own dignity and conscious of its own value, not only for the mother and child, but also for the Church and for society. The goal is a motherhood that is not seen as a pushback from women's advancement, but is embraced as an aid in its movement forward. The goal is no longer to leave motherhood behind, but to recover and appropriate it for the fulfillment of the women who are called to it.

The way you and I are going to achieve that goal is to take a fresh look at motherhood and see it in all its beautiful worth, through the reflections in these chapters. We are going to address your fears about motherhood: that it will cost you doing something really great with your life; that it will keep you from finding what is really meaningful; that you will not be a good mother; that you will have to endure many sacrifices — financial, physical, and professional. We will address these fears as I make a case that motherhood is an extraordinary vocation not to be forced into but to be accept wholeheartedly, because the adjustments motherhood may require of you are well worth the cost. The net result is a happier you and a healthier culture.

As you reflect on the beauty of this vocation, this book will help you in your personal discovery of the way you are uniquely called as a mother. Each woman's personal discovery will, indeed, differ from that of others. Throughout this book, I deliberately refer to many kinds of mothers, including adoptive mothers, stepmothers, spiritual mothers, unwed mothers, mothers who have had miscarriages, mothers who struggle with infertility, and those who struggle with hyper-fertility.

No one sets out thinking, *I will be unable to conceive*, or *I'm going to be an unwed mother*. Having had several miscarriages myself and having a sister who has not yet been able to carry a child to full term, but is a thriving, beautiful, adoptive mother, I can say that motherhood manifests itself differently in different women's lives. I am in awe of how sacred and holy this vocation is in the many ways it realizes itself, often through hardship. Yet always, in all its manifold diversity, motherhood gives glory to God. It is important that we all imagine motherhood not only or primarily as biological motherhood, but that we make room for the many kinds of motherhood as equally valuable and precious in the sight of God.

Before we proceed, I would like to say a word of caution about a particularly sensitive topic related to motherhood that I discuss in the pages ahead — namely, pregnancy. Pregnancy brings new life and joy, and it can also be a source of tremendous pain and loss. If you are in a place in your life where you prefer not to read about pregnancy — if you are experiencing grief, perhaps due to miscarriage, long-term infertility, the loss of a child, or other possible tragedies relating to pregnancy and childbirth — this might not be the right time to read this book. This book intentionally celebrates pregnancy and childbirth. That said, this book equally celebrates and honors women who struggle with infertility as well as stepmothers and adoptive mothers. Perhaps, rather than not reading this book right now, choosing to read it will actually help you, as you come to see many expressions of motherhood lifted up and celebrated. Only you can say what is right for you at this time. If you are experiencing deep pain that you bear as a daily cross, I honor your suffering. I passionately believe that God has a beautiful design for your life. In the end, may we all be able to celebrate the diverse array of mothers in the world. May we be united under our common mission and by the very significant title of "mother."

ॐ

Each of the following chapters focuses on a theme that is essential to every mother's interior development as she contemplates the role of motherhood in her life. The first chapter, "The Dignity of Motherhood," takes a look at the biblical foundations of the dignity of motherhood from the vantage point of Pope Saint John Paul II. Chapter 2, "Making Your Life a Masterpiece," reflects on the extraordinary power of freedom, helps you focus on the yearnings of your heart, and will equip you to make sincere and even daring life choices. Chapter 3, "Being Happy in the Face of Death," takes up the theme of achieving human fulfillment, promoting the idea that personhood culminates in its ability to love. The fourth chapter, "How to Flourish," examines the career-or-home question and makes the case that, for both working mothers and stay-at-home mothers, motherhood does not hold women back from doing really great things with their lives. Chapter 5, "Becoming a Radical Christian," takes a look at the spiritual genius of motherhood and helps women find their true path to God, even if for the first time. The final chapter, "Mothers as World Changers," presents the many ways mothers build, shape, and strengthen society and why both working mothers and stay-at-home moms make a significant, irreplaceable contribution to our world.

Each chapter has four sections. First, the themes are developed with insights from theologians, saints, and philosophers throughout the ages. Each theme will help you become better able to embrace motherhood — its significance, purpose, and worth. Second, each chapter will explore "The Art of Motherhood." Each of us is called to be an artist, tasked with designing our lives using God's gifts. We will explore art and architecture to serve as metaphors for this creative design. Third, each chapter includes "The Prayer of Motherhood," a spiritual prayer, tool, or insight that will help you in your holy work of discernment and living out your vocation. Finally, the "Questions for Reflection" at the end of each chapter will help you apply the chapter's material to your life, either on your own or in a group study.

Together, we will look at the prospects for happiness, meaning, and spiritual depth that await us in motherhood. My hope and prayer for you as you read this book is twofold: First, that you will discover the genius of motherhood and enter this vocation or re-engage with it with new awareness of its meaning, beauty, and power; and second, that the dignity of women and motherhood in all its forms will become fully appreciated by our churches and our world, for the sake not only of women, but of the churches and culture that are in a deficit without a complete appreciation of femininity. Let us become leaders and world changers by taking up the mantle of motherhood.

THE DIGNITY OF MOTHERHOOD

Is there some part of you that desires to be a mother? Maybe it is buried, like a seed, deep inside; or maybe the desire is strong, vital, and well-established. If you are already a mother, how has this role integrated with the rest of who you are? Has it been the flowering of who you feel you are meant to be, or has it caused a dormancy in the other plans that are essential to your flourishing as a person? Has it come easily or only after long waiting and struggle? For most women, at least some part of them yearns to be a mother: to carry a baby inside them, to hold a child in their arms, to feel the love and experience the intimacy that only mothers experience.

Despite the fact that part of you has this desire, motherhood can present a challenge to your twenty-first-century life. You may have reasons not to prioritize motherhood. In all likelihood, it does not advance your career, income, or personal interests. It does not impress the professionals in your life — in fact, it is something you almost wish you could hide from them. In these senses, it may be impractical or complicating.

Even deeper than that, you may be biased against motherhood as unsophisticated. Animals and insects reproduce. Mammals rear their young. Women have finally been given the opportunity to do something more than mate and nurture, so shouldn't you back-burner what we have in common with other animals and focus all your energies on developing what is specifically human about you? Shouldn't you actualize the highest potencies you have?

Let us first explore the Christian message that motherhood is a vocation of great dignity, by way of John Paul II's theological and scriptural reflections on motherhood. John Paul II shows more clearly than any Christian theologian, in my view, the biblical basis for the dignity of motherhood. I can honestly say that, as the product of New York City feminism, I am the Catholic mother I am today because of him. Let me share with you my personal experience of becoming a mother, as well as the view I have come to develop of the varied ways in which motherhood can employ a human being's highest faculties. In "The Art of Motherhood," we will look at Henri Matisse as an inspiration for finding dignity in the world around us, including in our vocations as mothers. Then in "The Prayer of Motherhood," we will pray with *lectio divina* on the scriptural passage in which Mary is called to motherhood.

JOHN PAUL II ON THE CHRISTIAN BASIS OF THE DIGNITY OF MOTHERHOOD

John Paul II sees in Christianity a dignified understanding of motherhood. That dignity is grounded in the creation narrative in Genesis. He writes: "Before creating man, the Creator withdraws into himself, in order to seek the pattern and inspiration in the mystery of his Being, which is already disclosed here as the divine 'We.'"[1] With a view to this mystery of the divine "We," God creates male and female human beings: "God created man in his own image, in the image of God he created him; male and female he created them" (Gn 1:27). As God looks to himself to see the pattern after which to create humanity, what he sees is *divine communion*: what the New Testament will more fully reveal as the Blessed Trinity. John Paul II poignantly articulates, "God in his deepest mystery is not a solitude but a family."[2] What does it mean, then, for humankind to be made in the image of God? In addition to meaning that we are rational and free creatures capable of knowing God and loving him, it also means we are designed to exist in relationship — first, that of a family.[3] Spousal love, motherhood, and fatherhood are the original meaning, according to John Paul II, of what it is for a human being to be made in the image of God.

The pope highlights the biblical message that motherhood is a gift.[4] Sarah, for example, had been unable to conceive well into her old age. Yet God promised to bless her and give her a child: God said, "I will bless her, and she shall be a mother of nations; kings of peoples shall come from her" (Gn 17:16). Rachel, too, suffered from the lack of a child and then was honored with the birth of her son Joseph, who would become a great ruler under the pharaoh of Egypt. Note that many of the most significant women in Scripture struggle with infertility. It is as though God proclaims through their lives: *Each human life is precious! Family is precious! Motherhood is precious!*

If you are a woman who has not yet been able to conceive or bear a child, consider how God might use you as a modern prophet. Our age is marked by what John Paul II calls "the culture of death," a pro-choice, anti-family culture that disparages both human life and motherhood. As you grieve the lack of a child, perhaps God is inviting you to be a "sign of contradiction" (again, a term used by John Paul II) to the culture, praying a prayer in your heart that breathes into our world a message of truth about the value of family and human life.

Hannah desired a child with all her heart, and when God gave her a son, she exclaimed: "My heart exults in the LORD; / my strength is exalted in the LORD" (1 Sm 2:1). Mary, echoing Hannah, sings out, "My soul magnifies the Lord, and my spirit rejoices in God my Savior, for he has regarded the low estate of his handmaiden. For behold, henceforth all generations will call me blessed" (Lk 1:46–48). These and other mothers in Scripture rejoice in the gift of a child. The prayer of a woman yearning for a child is powerful: All of these women became mothers of people who changed the course of history and the landscape of God's kingdom. Whether you have a prolonged wait to have a child or are never able to conceive, Scripture conveys the message that a mother who longs to bear a child is specially chosen, and her prayers are a significant force in the kingdom of God.

These and other mothers in Scripture are chosen instruments in God's providential plan. As queen mother, for example, Bathsheba influences her son, King Solomon (see

1 Kgs 2:19–20). When she enters the room, Solomon bows down to her and invites her to sit on a throne. She makes a request, and he accomplishes it. At the wedding feast at Cana, Mary plays a decisive role in the timing of Jesus' first miracle. She tells her Son that the wedding hosts have no wine. He replies, "What have you to do with me? My hour has not yet come." Mary says to the servants, "Do whatever he tells you." And Jesus proceeds with the miracle of changing water into wine (Jn 2:1–11). These are women who, precisely in their motherhood, cooperate with and help to bring about God's will for Israel.

Regarding the motherhood and fatherhood of human persons, John Paul II highlights their spiritual significance. What makes a family a family, in his view, is most fundamentally its reflection of God. He argues that, for those who become biological parents, the procreation of their children is more than a matter of cells and hormones. He says that, although other species "multiply," for humans, this word is used in the Bible in an analogous sense.[5] "Human fatherhood and motherhood, while remaining biologically similar to that of other living beings in nature, contain in an essential and unique way a 'likeness' to God which is the basis of the family as a community of human life, as a community of persons united in love (*communio personarum*)."[6] John Paul II asserts that the procreation of children is properly understood in terms of a community of love among persons, containing in an essential way a likeness to the communion of the Divine Persons. He underscores the point: "We wish to emphasize that God himself is present in human fatherhood and motherhood quite differently than he is present in all other instances of begetting 'on earth.'" John Paul II highlights motherhood in particular as bearing a reflection of the triune God: "On the human level, can there be any other 'communion' comparable to that between a mother and a child whom she has carried in her womb and then brought to birth?"[7]

We have here an awe-inspiring message about motherhood: It is fundamentally and most essentially a reflection of the Trinity. Motherhood is not merely biological: It is spiritual as well. This spiritual dimension carries over to all kinds of motherhood. Being a stepmother, an adoptive mother, a foster mother, as well as a godmother, grandmother, or spiritual mother — each vocation has what is most essentially true about motherhood, according to John Paul II: It bears a reflection of the Blessed Trinity, a communion of persons united in love.

In the New Testament, too, motherhood is dignified beyond mere biology. Christ himself links motherhood to the paschal mystery. He likens his death on the cross to a mother in childbirth, and then his resurrection to a mother with her newborn child in her arms. "When a woman is in labor, she has pain, because her hour has come; but when she is delivered of the child, she no longer remembers the anguish, for joy that a child is born into the world." Continuing, Jesus uses the image of a new mother to depict the joy his disciples will have when he is raised from the dead: "So you have sorrow now, but I will see you again and your hearts will rejoice, and no one will take your joy from you" (Jn 16:21–22). Perhaps the greatest possible human experience, the joy of beholding the Resurrection of Christ from the dead, is described in terms of the joy of motherhood. A woman's motherhood is a paschal sign.[8] Here again, John Paul II goes beyond nature and highlights a spiritual meaning in motherhood. Might we not reflect further that an adoptive mother, too, may hold an infant in her arms, after the long agony of childlessness? Or bring an older child into her home after many years of longing for parenthood? Does she not, too, experience a joy that reflects the pascal mystery? Scripture gives us permission to see in the vocation of motherhood — I believe in all its forms — the holy pattern of the death and resurrection of Christ.

Not only does motherhood have a special dignity, according to Scripture, but one mother, Mary, is the greatest of all human beings in relation to her Son; she is the high point of creation after Christ.[9] "When the time had fully come, God sent forth his Son, born of woman" (Gal 4:4). Paul's words locate a mother — at the time, an unwed mother — at the central point of salvation history.[10] This great event occurs when Mary gives her consent to the angel Gabriel, who has announced God's invitation to her to be the mother of the Messiah. Mary's response is: "Behold, I am the handmaid of the Lord; let it be to me according to your word" (Lk 1:38). Mary's expression "Let it be" in Latin is *fiat*. And so, through the ages, scholars have referred to Mary's *fiat* as her choice, her act of the will, that said yes to God's plan.

John Paul II comments that Mary's consent to become the mother of the Son of God is crucial for all of humanity. He quotes Vatican II:

> People look to the various religions for answers to those profound mysteries of the human condition which, today, even as in olden times, deeply stir the human heart: What is a human being? What is the meaning and purpose of life? ... Where lies the path to true happiness? What is the truth about death, judgment and retribution beyond the grave? What, finally,

is that ultimate and unutterable mystery which en-
gulfs our being, and from which we take our origin
and towards which we move?[11]

Through all the ages, from ancient times to the present, John
Paul II affirms, there have been various peoples who had dif-
fering conceptions of that hidden power that is present in the
course of things and in the events of human life; some people
have recognized it as a Supreme Being or a Divinity. Against
this backdrop of the human heart in search of God, John Paul
II says, Scripture tells us that in the fullness of time, God gives
the response: God the Father sends his Son. God's answer to
the questions of the human heart is his very self, his Son, one
in substance with the Father. "This self-revelation is salvific in
character."[12] In his goodness, God chose to reveal himself in the
Son, and by him man has access to the Father in the Holy Spirit
and comes to share in the Divine Nature. "A woman is to be
found at the center of this salvific event," John Paul II writes.[13]
The self-revelation of God is outlined in the Annunciation. "Do
we not find in the Annunciation at Nazareth the beginning of
that definitive answer by which God himself 'attempts to calm
people's hearts'?"[14] John Paul II sees Mary's motherhood as
fundamental to God's answer to the metaphysical and spiritual questions that have always beset humanity, because through
her motherhood, God reveals the answers that culminate in
Christ. Mary's motherhood is central to the salvific event.

By her yes to God's invitation to motherhood, and through
her motherhood, Mary becomes "the archetype of the human
race." John Paul II writes:

The dignity of the "woman" [Galatians 4:4] … consists in the supernatural elevation to union with God in Jesus Christ, which determines the ultimate finality of the existence of every person both on earth and in eternity. From this point of view, the "woman" is the representative and the archetype of the whole human race: she represents the humanity which belongs to all human beings, both men and women.[15]

Mary is the exemplar of all humans, both men and women, because her will was perfectly united with God's. The union of Mary with God is a pure grace and gift of the Holy Spirit through her Immaculate Conception:

At the same time, however, through her response of faith Mary exercises her free will and thus fully shares with her personal and feminine "I" in the event of the Incarnation. With her "*fiat*" Mary becomes the authentic subject of that union with God which was realized in the mystery of the Incarnation of the Word, who is of one substance with the Father.[16]

In other words, it is through her free will that, in her uniquely feminine way, Mary enters into perfect union with God and thus shows all human beings how to be a Christian.

&

The Bible gives us many reasons to posit that the human mother has a value far beyond simple reproduction and survival of the fittest. Rather, the dignity of human motherhood is grounded in its reflection of divine life. As we have seen, the motherhood of Mary is central to the salvific event and God's sovereign plan. Consequently, all human motherhood has been elevated through Christ.

How do these theological reflections impact you? Christianity casts a vision of the dignity of motherhood that is far beyond the reproduction of other kinds of animals. This vision may help you, as it helped me, to be willing to say yes to motherhood and give your own kind of *fiat* to this vocation.

A LARGER VISION OF MOTHERHOOD

(If you would prefer not to hear a story about pregnancy, you may want to skip this personal anecdote in the next few paragraphs and pick up in the section after the flower icon.)

One morning at dawn, I burst out of the bathroom with a pregnancy test in my hands. I showed Ron the unmistakable two pink lines in the result window. We checked and rechecked the instruction sheet, which indicated that two pink lines mean "pregnant." We jumped up and down and shouted with joy. As the sun rose, we beheld the stick in all its splendor. It was one of the choicest, richest moments of my life, and I was bursting with new, maternal pride.

After Ron departed for work, I settled cross-legged on the bed, propped up with pillows behind my back, my Bible in my lap, my journal by my side, and my rosary in my hand. As the soft light shone through the windows, I began my morning prayers. I had enjoyed a daily prayer life since becoming a Christian at age sixteen, but that day, I had a special eagerness to pray and share my heart with God. I longed to thank him for having blessed me with this new human life in my womb. I longed to talk with him about my excitement. I longed to reflect with him on this wondrous mystery. I longed to share with him my thoughts, feelings, fears, hopes, and dreams. Today would mark the beginning of a new kind of prayer for me: prayer as a mother, prayer for my child.

Soon my prayer turned toward the expectant Mary, and I pondered the almost unthinkable reality of her having Christ, the Son of God, inside her. I imagined her interior life: What did Mary think? How did she feel? What physical changes were taking place in her body? I was overcome with the sense of the dignity of her new state. She was now an expectant mother, and this was not just perpetuation of the species. This was not reducible to cells and hormones. Mary was called by God to be the model for all humanity, the exemplar of the human person in relation to God; and it was precisely through her yes to motherhood that she would be exalted.

In twenty years of motherhood, I have come to believe that motherhood is not mere procreation and instinct. Motherhood can and should be seen as so much more. We can see motherhood through various lenses that begin to uncover the richness of the vocation, to reveal it as a vocation that can engage a person's most sophisticated capacities. First, motherhood can be understood artistically. That is, human mothers can think about their vocation and design it in ways unique to them. Much like a painter who develops her own style on the canvas, a human mother can bring her personal touch to the kind of mother she wants to be. As John Paul II says, "All men and women are entrusted with the task of crafting their own life: in a certain sense, they are to make of it a work of art, a masterpiece."[17] Mothers can reflect on their vocation and design their lives with intentionality. I will be drawing on artists in each chapter of this book and going into depth on this theme in chapter 2, to provide you with inspiration as you artistically develop your motherhood.

Second, motherhood can be understood metaphysically. It can be considered in light of the nature of the human person and in light of questions such as: What does it mean to be a person? What is the meaning of human life? What is human excellence? These and other metaphysical questions can be examined from the perspective of motherhood. We are going to look more deeply into these questions in chapters 2 through 4. How can motherhood help a person achieve human goals, achieve excellence, and fulfill the longings of the human soul?

Third, motherhood can be understood spiritually. Just as a woman who chooses to become a Discalced Carmelite makes choices that deliberately model her life on Christ, so can a Christian, and a Catholic Christian in particular, choose to find union with Christ through her vocation as a mother. That will be the focus of chapter 5.

Fourth, motherhood can be understood sociologically. What impact do mothers have on our culture? Can mothers make a difference in the world? What kind of social roles and leverage do they have? How can it be optimized? Such questions can enhance one's awareness of the importance of her role as a mother. This will be the theme of chapter 6.

When considered from these dimensions, one begins to discover the dignity of motherhood. In the remainder of this book, my task will be to help you to identify the dignity of motherhood as it might apply to your life.

Henri Matisse, *The Dessert: Harmony in Red*

THE ART OF MOTHERHOOD: HENRI MATISSE AND DIGNITY

As you reflect on the role of motherhood in your life, consider Henri Matisse, a French artist at the turn of the twentieth century. Henri Matisse is an inspiration to me. Rather than depicting realistic renderings from real life, he painted still lifes, nudes, and portraits in a way that emphasizes massive bursts of color. His work says to me, "Just look at that blue. Have you ever seen such vibrant beauty?"

Additionally, Matisse seems to paint not exactly what he sees, but a depiction of his love for and experience of the subject matter. He portrays his experience of the dignity of his surroundings and the impact that these things have on him. It's as though his purposeful lack of the perspective and realism mastered by the Renaissance artists allows him to depict the interior experience he has. When I look at his paintings, I feel his ecstatic experience of the subject and its dignity, rather than his observation of the details he observed.

Look at Matisse's *The Dessert: Harmony in Red*. When I see this painting, which I consider one of his greatest masterpieces, I cannot help but feel that he is in love. A humble lady is setting a bowl of dessert on a little country table. Matisse is not in love with the lady or the dessert. He is not taken with the lavishness of the surroundings. Matisse is in love with life, with beauty itself. The raspberry red is his hymn to being alive. He is so intoxicated with beauty that the pattern of twisting vines on the tablecloth jumps off the fabric and climbs up the walls. Matisse is not creating an ode to nature, as the classical Greeks did. He has created an ode to experiencing beauty. He is saying, "Do you appreciate this the way I do? Behold it!" His work is a celebration of enjoying life, even in its humblest moments.

Matisse inspires us to become intentional about embracing the radiance of life and finding dignity where others may miss it. He urges us to craft lives that are punctuated with appreciation for what really has value. His goldfish paintings, his ladies surrounded by textiles, and his window views of palm trees send the message: Notice the beauty all around you. Stop being so busy. Remember what is most important in life. Capture the loveliness in whatever way you can. Let beauty show itself to you in the most mundane of places.

Matisse began painting when he was recovering from an illness. His mother brought him paint supplies. Matisse says that he discovered "a kind of paradise within" when he painted.[18] He depicted the paradise all around him in common things and, in the process, created an interior paradise.

I invite you to think of vocations in this way. Wouldn't it be wonderful for your vocation to create a paradise within you? To bring you peace, delight, and joy? At its most sublime, the vocation of motherhood — whether you have recently adopted a baby or have just sent a child to college or have just become a grandmother — can be marked by a steady sense of wonder at the dignity of one's children, spouse, and loved ones. The highest form of motherhood is for it to be a little taste of heaven on earth.

Matisse's approach came hard to him. He rebelled against the masters of his sophisticated art school in Paris. Having studied the classical realistic style and copied some of the greatest works of art, he abandoned this path and created an entirely new style of art. Inspired by Vincent Van Gogh, Paul Cezanne, and the Pointillists, Matisse replaced realistic figures and their intricate detail with flat surfaces and broad lines. His portrait of his wife is called *The Green Line* because a large green brush stroke runs through her eyebrows (poor lady!). Matisse was called a "wild beast" by the art critics in Paris. They meant to attack him, but this name served as a launch point for a new movement in art, Fauvism (*les fauves* means "wild beasts").

It can take courage to choose family life. To enjoy and celebrate the simple things of life can require rebellion and garner severe criticism from others — as Matisse received from the art critics in Paris. Does your heart yearn for a child? This is sacred. This is paradise. It may not win the applause of the professionals in your life, but consider bucking the system, rebelling against the conventions that are attempting to dictate your future. Take control of your own path and do not fear. In upcoming chapters, we will consider many options: full-time and part-time employment outside the home, as well as full-time employment in the home and variations on these themes. Each one has merits and could be right for you. In the meantime, commit to celebrating love and satisfying the deepest desires of your heart.

PRAYER OF A MOTHER:
LECTIO DIVINA WITH THE ANNUNCIATION

We have talked about the dignity of the vocation of motherhood. One tool that might help you discern how motherhood fits into the overall picture of your life is to pray over the Annunciation using a form of prayer called *lectio divina*. As we have seen in the Annunciation, the angel Gabriel announced to Mary that she would conceive a Son who would be the Messiah. It is perhaps the quintessential scriptural passage about the dignity of motherhood, and Mary is the quintessential woman and mother. I encourage you to develop a relationship with her and foster it as you develop in your femininity and contemplate the vocation of motherhood. Praying the Rosary is a wonderful way to do this.[19] Additionally, reading the Scriptures prayerfully, especially through *lectio divina*, can greatly enhance your awareness of and love for Our Lady.

Lectio divina is a way of meditating on a Scripture passage that helps it become more alive to you. The prayer format dates all the way back to AD 300, has been used by monks and nuns as well as the laity over the centuries, and has been recommended by Pope Saint John Paul II and Pope Emeritus Benedict XVI. Using *lectio divina*, you may hear the stirrings of your heart and the voice of God within you regarding the dignity of the vocation of motherhood.

Let us begin the process now. *Lectio divina* has four steps: reading, meditation or use of the imagination, vocal and mental prayer, and contemplation. Open with a prayer, something like, "Holy Spirit, open my heart to your presence, your love, and your guidance. I love you."

1. Reading

Read the following passage, not for the purpose of study or intellectual understanding, but to let God speak to your heart. God's Word is just that: his words to you, his way of speaking directly to you. Read slowly, dwelling on each word or phrase and pausing before you go to the next one. Look for any way God wants to tell you something. You might want to jot down in a notebook any thoughts, impressions, or feelings you may have.

> In the sixth month [of Elizabeth's pregnancy] the angel Gabriel was sent from God to a city of Galilee named Nazareth, to a virgin betrothed to a man whose name was Joseph, of the house of David; and the virgin's name was Mary. And he came to her and said, "Hail, full of grace, the Lord is with you!" But she was greatly troubled at the saying, and considered in her mind what sort of greeting this might be. And the angel said to her, "Do not be afraid, Mary, for you have found favor with God. And behold, you will conceive in your womb and bear a son, and you shall call his name Jesus.
>
> > He will be great, and will be called the Son of the Most High;
> > and the Lord God will give to him the throne of his father David,
> > and he will reign over the house of Jacob for ever;

and of his kingdom there will be no end."

And Mary said to the angel, "How can this be, since I have no husband?" And the angel said to her,

"The Holy Spirit will come upon you,
and the power of the Most High will overshadow you;
therefore the child to be born will be called holy,
the Son of God.

And behold, your kinswoman Elizabeth in her old age has also conceived a son; and this is the sixth month with her who was called barren. For with God nothing will be impossible." And Mary said, "Behold, I am the handmaid of the Lord; let it be to me according to your word." And the angel departed from her. (Luke 1:26–38)

2. Meditation

Use your imagination to mediate on this scene. Place yourself in it. Maybe you are Mary or Gabriel. What are you feeling? What are you thinking? What is important to learn, understand, or say right now? Let the Holy Spirit speak to you through your imagination. Both Saint Teresa of Ávila and Saint Ignatius of Loyola are famous for promoting the use of the imagination in prayer. Imagine the floor, the lighting, the surroundings. What scents do you smell? What sounds do you hear? What fabrics or materials do you touch? What time of day or night is it? Is anyone else close by?

3. Prayer

Take this time to have a conversation with God. In your mind, out loud, or on paper, speak to God. Let him speak to you. What does he want to communicate to you? What is your response? Notice that Mary's first response to Gabriel is her expressing the problem she sees with Gabriel's message: How can she be with child if she has never known a man? Likewise, share your reservations or clarifying questions with God. Then, notice that Mary's second response is her *fiat*, her choice to accept God's will: "Let it be to me according to your word," or in other translations, "Let it be done to me according to your will."

What is God's will for you? What is your answer? Be honest and ask for grace from God. Mary is full of grace, and it takes grace to unite our will with God's. Take time to consider where you are right now in your discernment process, and ask for help in your next steps.

4. Contemplation

Take time to sit with God. No more talking. No more working or striving. It is time to just *be with him*. He loves for us to sit in his presence and enjoy his companionship. This can be hard to do, since we are so used to *doing* something. When your mind wanders, gently remind yourself that the Lord is present and just smile at him. Let him receive you back, and try once again to lovingly be with him.

Conclude with a short prayer, such as: Lord, thank you for being with me. Thank you for loving me. Thank you for desiring intimacy with me. Please deepen my relationship with you and with Mary, my mother. Please stay by my side and speak your truth to me. Guide me in my ways and make my life pleasing to you. Fashion it so that it will bring glory to you. Amen.

Once your *lectio divina* is complete, you may want to take out a notebook and write down any thoughts or experiences you had. Go back to your writing from time to time as you continue praying and discerning. Use your notebook to answer the following questions. May God bring you clarity, peace, and renewal.

QUESTIONS FOR REFLECTION

1. How were you raised to think about motherhood?
2. What is your reaction to John Paul II's theological view of motherhood as elevated by Christ?
3. Does it resonate with you that we can bring artistic design to motherhood? Are you open to looking deeper into metaphysical, spiritual, and sociological questions about the meaning of life and eternity as they pertain to motherhood?
4. How does the work of Henri Matisse affect you? Which of his works is your favorite? Have you cultivated the practice of noticing the dignity of your surroundings? Do you live life too quickly and functionally, or are you good at stopping and delighting in the beauty of the world around you?
5. How did you find the *lectio divina* prayer experience? What is your main takeaway from your time in prayer?
6. Describe at this point how you feel about motherhood: Excited? Nervous? Both? Other feelings?

— 2 —

MAKING YOUR LIFE
A MASTERPIECE

Having gotten a glimpse of the dignity of mother-hood, let's now consider how it can be a signifi-cant part of your successful life as a woman in the twen-ty-first century. The goal I am identifying in this book is how to bring about a culture that fully appreciates motherhood, and accommodates all the ways a woman might creatively pursue motherhood as well as her other interests, if she feels the need or the calling to do so. This chapter will help you engage your best, most earnest dis-cernment in identifying your particular calling.

Do you have an education? An employable skill? Do you have some professional or personal endeavor you en-joy? Do you have a desire to contribute to the society or church to which you belong? If you have an interest outside the home, does it compete with having children in the home? Are you worried that you will not be able to do both well? Do you fear failure? Some women will make the choice to work full-time; others will take gaps from their careers to be home with young children; some will work part-time while having young children; still others will choose to stay home with their children for the long term and sacrifice much or all of their professional lives.

You have the chance to become an artist and use your highest powers of creativity and intelligence as you thoughtfully design your life. You have a shot at expressing your personal, unique style by making a masterpiece. The artist acts in the image of God in fashioning a work of beauty. As John Paul II says:

> Through his "artistic creativity" man appears more than ever "in the image of God," and he accomplishes this task above all in shaping the wondrous "material" of his own humanity and then exercising creative dominion over the universe which surrounds him. … With loving regard, the divine Artist passes on to the human artist a spark of his own surpassing wisdom, calling him to share in his creative power.[1]

Mothers can access their highest faculties and, in reflecting on their vocation and designing their lives, enjoy the creative power of God.

To engage with your creative power, the first task is to find your freedom. When Michelangelo was preparing to sculpt a statue of David, he had many choices as to how to depict this

Old Testament figure: Would he represent David as small or large in stature? Would he depict him before, during, or after David's flinging the stone at Goliath? What emotion or state of mind in David would he capture? Michelangelo had full freedom to imagine and contemplate the design of his statue. His decisions were so novel and timely for the culture in which he lived that his *David* in Florence is one of the most celebrated works of art of all time.

Each of us has freedom, but many of us never discover or utilize it. In fact, in the ancient world, so few people experienced the use of their freedom that it was one of the great appeals of Christianity to the ancient people:

> It is difficult for us to imagine the disturbance [the notion of humanity's dignity and worth] created in the soul of man in the ancient world. At the first tidings of them humanity was lifted on a wave of hope. … Man was freed, in his own eyes, from the ontological slavery with which Fate burdened him. … It was mankind as a whole that found its night suddenly illumined and took cognizance of its royal liberty.[2]

In the earliest decades of the Church, the message that we have freedom was one reason why Christianity became so popular. For most people in ancient times, although the problem endured for some through the present time, their freedom was dormant. They were told what kind of life they would live and they followed suit. Whether it was the child of a merchant in ancient Rome, the child of a miller in the Middle Ages, or the child of a middle-class family in the twenty-first century, many people grow up and do what they are expected to do. They marry the kind of person who fits into the world in which they find themselves, and they live every day of their lives basically within the parameters laid out for them.

Christianity heralds a new message, which is that we have freedom. This is why there is such an intense feeling of gladness radiating from the writings of the early Church.[3] Neither blind destiny nor fate controls our lives; God has revealed a way forward which is marked by freedom to choose God, to choose Christ, and to choose to participate in the eternal state of our souls. The Christian notion of freedom is *freedom for*: We are free to choose the highest and infinite good, which is God. We have the ability to deliberate how best to love and serve God.

This is contrary to the modern secular notion of freedom, which posits a complete and radical self-determination. The secular view of freedom says, for example, that I may decide to do whatever I want, whenever I want, and to whatever end. The Christian notion of freedom opposes this view, since Christianity recognizes us as *creatures*. We are creatures who are made by God and for God. We have freedom to choose God, but also the freedom to choose a lesser good (though to our own demise). When we choose what we are meant for, we become happy and we flourish. Alternatively, when we choose an inferior, finite good as our highest end, we become unhappy. To illustrate: If a pen is made to write, it should not choose (if it *could* choose) to spend its life acting like an eraser, or it would be forever frustrated. The Christian view says, "You are a creature made for God, and you have the gift of freedom to choose God." The secular view says, "You are a god of your own universe. Be anything you want; do anything you want." The problem is that when people make gods out of themselves and behave recklessly and self-indulgently, they tend to harm themselves. Secular self-determination usually leads to loneliness and self-destruction. While the Christian view of freedom might seem more limited, it is grounded in the truth that we are not gods but creatures. As creatures, we have the opportunity to thrive and become the best creatures we can be, to flourish and find true happiness.

We just saw how Mary used her freedom to give her *fiat*, saying yes to God's plan for her and the salvation of human-kind. She is the model for all Christians, both men and wom-en, showing us how to say yes to God. How might you use your freedom in a way that is similarly powerful, that elevates your dignity, and that will help you artistically design your life in a way that is uniquely yours? In pursuing this question, let us consider Saint Margaret Mary Alacoque and the amazing story of her discovery of her freedom, and the choice to use it for God.

NOT FOR THE FAINT OF HEART: SAINT MARGARET MARY ALACOQUE

Born in France in the seventeenth century, Margaret lost her father when she was very young and lived with her moth-er and three brothers. As a young girl, she felt called to be-come a nun. But as she grew, she found pleasure in childlike things, and after a serious illness, she said, "I thought only of seeking pleasure in the enjoyment of my liberty, without concerning myself much about the fulfillment of my prom-ise."[4] She found delight in her liberty, or freedom, which she imagined might be threatened by religious life.

A sad turn of events occurred when her mother fell into disrepute and her mother-in-law, sister-in-law, and aunt took over the family home. Margaret and her mother were treated like servants and dealt with harshly. Christ appeared to Margaret, and said that he desired to be the absolute Master of her heart. Margaret had a profound conversion at this time and felt the consolation of the suffering Christ with her at all times, joining her sufferings to his.

Margaret's worst sufferings, however, were those caused by her mother. Her mother suffered at the hands of the women of the house, and endured a life-threatening illness that caused swelling in her head. Even after her recovery, she was a constant source of agony for Margaret. As Margaret got older, several young men presented themselves as suitors for her. Margaret wanted to become a nun, but her mother insisted that she marry:

> My relations pressed me to accept; and my mother, incessantly weeping, told me that she looked to me as her only hope of putting an end to her misery by joining me as soon as I should be settled in the world. … The devil especially took advantage of the tender affection which I had for my mother, and unceasingly representing to me the tears she shed, suggesting she would die of grief if I became a nun and that … I would be responsible for her death.[5]

In fact, no fewer than four times in her autobiography, Margaret mentions her mother's accusation that Margaret's becoming a nun would be the reason for her mother's death, and that Margaret would have to account for this death before God.[6]

Not only were Margaret's choices threatened by pressure from her mother, but Margaret also says that she feared becoming a nun because "she dreaded renouncing her liberty."[7] Even if it were in order to fast and pray in whatever manner she chose, her liberty was precious to her, and she feared losing it. Then, when she finally convinced her brother, who was mainly in charge of her, that she was to become a nun, he insisted that she enter the Ursuline Order, to which their beloved cousin belonged. Margaret then endured a several-year battle with her family members, including this cousin, who pressured her to join the Ursulines. During the course of this battle, Margaret had another moment of conversion, in which she used her liberty in the most sublime way:

> One day after receiving Communion [Jesus] showed me that he was the most beautiful, the wealthiest, the most powerful, the most perfect, and the most accomplished among all lovers. … While he was speaking he spread such a great calm over my interior and filled my soul with such deep grace, that I resolved henceforth to die rather than to change. It then seemed to me that my bonds were broken and that I had nothing more to fear. … The Divine Spouse of my soul fearing lest I should escape him, asked me whether, considering my weakness, I would agree to his taking possession [of] and making himself Master of my liberty. I willingly consented, and from that time forth he took such a firm hold of my liberty that I never more enjoyed the use of it.[8]

Eventually Margaret persuaded her brother and petitioned for admission to the Order of the Visitation, also called the Holy Marys.

Upon entering the convent of the Holy Marys in Paray-le-Monial, Margaret writes, "It appeared to me that I was like a slave who sees herself released from her prison and chains, in order that she may enter the house of her Spouse to enjoy, without reserve, his presence, his wealth and his love."[9] Her chains, especially the pressures from her family, who had many diverse plans for her, were broken, and she was free to love God and serve him as she felt called.

Once in the convent, Margaret recounted the supernatural joy of many consolations from God, but was reproved by the other sisters, who said that "extraordinary ways" were not suitable for the daughters of Holy Mary. Margaret experienced confusion that Jesus would come to her in ways not permitted in the cloister. She requested that Jesus suspend all supernatural graces to her so that she could submit to her superiors. He asked in reply that she renew the sacrifice she had already made to him of her liberty and her whole being. She did so, provided that he would suspend the special graces. Jesus replied, "Fear nothing, my daughter, leave all to me, for I will constitute myself the Guardian of them and render thee powerless to resist me."[10] She gave Christ her liberty once again, even without his promise to suspend special graces.

Not long thereafter, praying before the Blessed Sacrament, she had the most extraordinary grace yet: "I was wholly penetrated with that Divine Presence. ... He made me repose for a long time upon his Sacred Breast, where he disclosed to me the marvels of his love and the inexplicable secrets of his Sacred Heart."[11]

Christ said to her: "My Divine Heart is so inflamed with the love of men, and for thee in particular that, being unable any longer to contain within itself the flames of its burning charity, it must needs spread them abroad by thy means, and manifest itself to mankind."[12] Here began Margaret's visions of the Sacred Heart of Jesus, which became the foundation of a new devotion, lasting through the present time. Margaret's extraordinary visions made history as she became the foundress of the devotion to the Sacred Heart of Jesus, which continues to blossom and enliven the hearts of the faithful even today.

From beginning to end, Margaret Mary Alacoque's story is one of a courageous woman finding her liberty in order to give it to God; to take up her freedom, especially over and against her mother and family, and even the sisters in her convent, in order to give it to Christ. When she gives the Absolute Master and Divine Spouse her freedom, only then does she experience true peace and complete calm. Only when, paradoxically, she uses her freedom to renounce her freedom to Christ does she engage in making a true masterpiece of her life, and become the fullness of who God wants her to be.

GREGORY OF NYSSA: FREEDOM AS SELF-DETERMINATION

The notion of freedom is an important part of the Christian tradition. One early Church Father who explored and developed the notion of freedom is Gregory of Nyssa (d. 386). Gregory of Nyssa was from a devout religious family. His mother, Emmelia, and her husband, Basil the Elder, are both saints, as is Gregory's grandmother, Saint Macrina the Elder. Emmelia and Basil the Elder had ten children, five of whom are saints recognized in both the Eastern Orthodox Churches and the Catholic Church: Basil the Great, Gregory of Nyssa, Peter of Sebaste, Naucratius, and Macrina the

Younger (who contributed significantly to the education of her brothers). Gregory of Nyssa, his brother Basil, and their friend Gregory of Nazianzus were the Cappadocian Fathers, who made an invaluable theological contribution by offering solutions to the Christological controversies of the time. They also had a decisive influence on the doctrine of the Trinity.

Gregory of Nyssa reflects on ways that the human person is made in the image of God. He highlights something akin to freedom, or liberty. He calls it "independence" and "self-determination." He writes, "Humanity was fully formed to the authentic image of the Son. For all the attributes we apply to the Son of God applied also to human beings: never-ending and blessed, independent and self-determining."[13] Gregory considers the question, "What does it mean to be made in the image of God?" He believes that the answer is the human capacity for self-determination. Human freedom for self-determination is a reflection of the divine image, and thus one of the most sublime aspects of the human person.

Again he writes: "He who made man to share in His own goodness and so equipped his nature with the means of acquiring everything excellent his desires might, in each case, correspond to that to which they were directed, would not have deprived him of the most excellent and precious blessings—I mean the gift of liberty and free will."[14] Gregory maintains that, if we did all things by necessity and were lacking in freedom, we would honor God only as a matter of servitude. Anything that participates in the divine, Gregory claims, has to be free so that "participation in the good may be the reward of virtue."[15]

Gregory's notion of freedom is one of *freedom for*, as I

described above: It is a freedom to love God freely and enter into communion with him as one reflecting the divine image. But this does not mean it is limited, or less than full, freedom. If it is a reflection of or participation in the divine freedom, nothing could be a more complete kind of freedom than that of God himself.

Reflecting on Gregory of Nyssa's notion of human freedom, we are right to recognize and engage it as one of the most precious, transcendent powers we have. As a mother or a potential mother, how might you use your freedom? To seek to have a first child? Or to be open to another child? To pursue adoption or foster parenting? Or, if you're a mother already, to consider adopting or fostering an additional child? Or might you discern that now is not the right time to bring another child into the world, or into your home? Our freedom is a mirror of the divine. It is exciting to use it prayerfully and, with the guidance of the Holy Spirit, to forge the unrepeatable, unique masterpiece of your life. Think back to Saint Margaret Mary Alacoque, whose liberty was constantly and vehemently threatened by her family members' pressure to marry and even to enter religious orders other than the one to which she felt called. Yet she could identify her liberty and she clung to it; she made the most precious gift she could to Christ, giving him her liberty. She chose the highest good, God, with this power that is a reflection of the divine image.

SAINT THOMAS AQUINAS: THE DIGNITY OF THE WILL

As we are considering the importance of finding your freedom and using it wisely, it may be helpful to reflect that only *persons* have freedom: God, angels, and human beings.

No other being in creation has it. Though animals display something akin to freedom, later theologians such as Saint Thomas Aquinas distinguished between sense appetite and the human will. Animals have appetites that lead them to finite things; for example, dogs follow the scent of bones, and cats pursue mice. Although, like animals, human beings have appetites, they also have intellects. While the lower appetites have as their proper object finite things (for example, your sensitive appetite is drawn to the juicy hamburger), your intellect, a power distinct from your sense appetite, has as its proper object *universals*, that is, forms of material objects in abstraction.

What is the will? The will is the power of the human soul that inclines toward what the intellect identifies as good. The will "follows upon the intellect."[16] This means that the will is a power, the power to choose what the intellect has deemed good. The intellect says, "Kale salads are healthful to eat," and the will follows and says, "I want a kale salad for lunch." Animals have certain senses that allow them to know where to safely build a nest, or that a predator is dangerous. For Aquinas, though, human rationality is altogether different. It has the power to know things *as such*. A human can write a whole treatise on how to find safe shelter or avoid predators. The will, following on the intellect, desires the good in general, not mere particular goods.

Can our wills be free? On the one hand, the will is by nature a faculty that desires the good in general. So, you could say it "necessarily" desires the good, and is not free to desire the bad in general. But for Aquinas, this is not a matter of coercion or restriction of freedom. This is just the very nature of the will. What it mainly desires is happiness or beatitude.

If our will desires the infinite good in general, and God is the infinite good, then in some sense, even if implicitly only, all people desire God.

But the will is free in another sense, according to Aquinas. It is free in terms of particular choices. Some particular goods are not necessary for human happiness, and the will is free to choose them or not. In this life, the human person does not always see the connection between God and happiness. So sometimes she chooses something inferior to God. The person can think that amassing great wealth will make her happy, but she is, in fact, wrong about that. Nevertheless, she can exercise her will to amass great wealth. She does so under the aspect of the good; but she does not always get right what will help her attain the infinite good.

Good training, positive influences, and informing one's conscience play parts here; we have to apply ourselves to learning what actually makes us happy, and hence the pursuit of wisdom is always applicable. Finding good role models, reading Scripture and the lives of the saints, going to confession, and participating in the sacraments and personal prayer all play important parts.

That said, we are free creatures. We have wills that work with and in response to our intellects, something animals do not have. We also have "free will," *liberum arbitrium*, which is our free choice regarding the means to the end. We have the power to deliberate whether this choice or that will make us happier. When Margaret Mary was deliberating between marriage to placate her mother and maintaining the vow that she made at a young age to God to become a nun, she was deliberating between two possible ways in which to serve God and others. Both are, objectively speaking, good choices. But she used her liberum arbitrium to respond to the voice within her that said, "Your true, God-given calling is to be a nun." She struggled with her will for many years, and sometimes her vision became cloudy. But in the end, she had the courage to make what was for her the unpopular choice, and follow her heart and God's personal call for her life.

Consequently, when we use our wills in freedom, we are acting higher than the animals. We are doing what only persons can do, and even when we face criticism or resistance for our choices, we should remember the dignity of our free will, especially when we use it wisely for the honor and love of God. Once again, it is always important to participate in the sacraments, to seek wise counsel, and to apply ourselves to God in prayer. But the highest and best path for each of us is to identify the best way for us personally to achieve happiness, and to have the courage to make use of our freedom for that path to beatitude.

The use of freedom is a privilege. It is the aspect of our nature that participates in the very freedom of God. Inevitably, God will call upon you to use your freedom in a way that pleases him, but does not please "the world." No truly happy person has ever coasted along, never having had to make hard choices. You become your best self (which, in a sense, is to become a saint) through those grace-filled, holy choices that define you. Your freedom is your power to make choices that no one else can dictate on your behalf or take away from you.

Do you feel the freedom to choose what you most want? Or do you feel as if your freedom has not found its voice yet? Do you have various voices that compete for attention in your mind? Do you feel that what you most want is in keeping with loving and serving God, or do you have some praying and spiritual reading to do? Your freedom, like your very life, is a treasure, a gift from God. May you, like Margaret Mary, identify your freedom and protect it.

Let me share with you my story of finding my true will and using my freedom as it applied to marriage and motherhood. Then, in the Art of Motherhood, we will take inspiration from Brunelleschi in the building of the largest dome in the world, followed by a tool for your discernment process taken from Saint Ignatius of Loyola's *Spiritual Exercises*.

DIZZYING LIFE CHOICES

I was sitting in a jazz club in Greenwich Village next to Ron Rombs, the cutest guy in graduate school. He had suggested that we share a cheese and fruit plate to go with our wine — a very smooth suggestion, I thought, for a first date. He asked me what my plans in life were and whether my aim was to be a professor of philosophy once I got my Ph.D. I said that I was considering a religious vocation and that I might become a nun.

Ron said to me: "Oh, that is so interesting! I spent many years thinking I would become a monk. I was seriously considering a monastic vocation."

"Well, do you not have one?" I probed.

He calmly and quietly said, "No, I discerned instead that I have a vocation to family."

I felt that sentence like a thundering wind, sweeping through my soul. A *vocation to family*? What a pickup line! I had never heard of such a thing. I had heard of a vocation to the priesthood or religious life; I had heard of vocations to a profession, such as a doctor or a lawyer. But I thought that a vocation is what one chooses *instead of* being primarily concerned with family life. Family life was mundane, I thought; it is *not* to choose as a vocation. A vocation, I believed, would be a call away from a focus on family.

Now, sitting next to this handsome man, my whole concept of vocation and family reoriented itself. Ron clearly loved God and wanted to give his life in service to him. And, rather than seeing family life as inferior to other great human pursuits, he saw it as a high calling, worthy of one's lifelong focus and devotion. I was weak and dizzy and began to fall in love with him at that moment.

After several months of dating, Ron and I talked seriously about getting married. One day, Ron told me he wanted to take me out for a special evening. I imagined that he might propose. I called my mom and said, "I think he is going to ask me to marry him. But, Mom, I thought I wanted to be a nun." She replied with wise words about finding true happiness and recognizing the passions of one's heart. She said my love for Ron was so strong, and that is what a wonderful marriage is made of.

I hung up and sat on my couch. I stared at the large, looming trees outside my Bronx apartment and listened to the wind rustling the leaves. I felt that I was on a huge precipice. My whole future was about to be determined. It had been wide open, replete with such wonderful and diverse possibilities. For them all to close in on one narrow path felt ominous. I found it hard to breathe. I was not sure I was ready for this level of finality. I felt a whirling sensation as my life flashed before me. Could I really choose marriage? Would I become a mother? Would I teach? What would my life look like? Would Ron make me happy? Would I make him happy? Did I really know him well enough? It had all happened so fast. Maybe he was not as smart or reliable or faithful as he seemed. How did I know that he would be trustworthy? Or that I would be trustworthy?

I wish I could say that I picked up a volume of Bonaventure or Aquinas and read about the freedom of the will. I wish I could say that I heard God's voice or saw a dove alight on a framed picture of Ron. I just sat there, scared.

But it was as though a voice, buried within me, rushed to the surface and said, "Say yes to Ron!" It was a powerful impulse, a force from deep inside that burst through the crust of opposition and all the clatter in my head. When this voice spoke, I felt alive.[17] I felt as if the real me was being given a rare moment to speak. All the other voices had to step aside and listen. There was a hush and wide stares. They watched, riveted, while the true me said, "I want to be genuinely happy. I want to live large and become fully who God wants me to be. I want to give my all to someone … but not just anyone … *to Ron*. This is my most daring, authentic, honest, sincerely loving decision. I want to be with this man because he is beautiful, gentle, faithful, and kind. I want to be married to this Catholic man who has a *vocation to family* because I believe that I, too, have a vocation to family. I want to give our marriage and family everything I've got."

The doorbell rang. Before I knew it, Ron and I were in Manhattan at the Bethesda Fountain under the large, white moon, with Ron kneeling down on one knee, asking me to marry him. I said yes and put on the stylish ring he had bought with the little money he had. I could see in his eyes how nervously excited he was, how monumental this was for him. He looked as dizzy as I felt. I realized that both of us might be ruining our lives. Then again, we might be making the most brilliant decision we ever would. That was the gamble, and there was no one there to tell us how it would turn out.

I knew that the choice to marry Ron meant the choice to be open to having children. As though out of nowhere, secret, suppressed desires to have a home, and yes, even to have children, began coming to the surface. I was aware that balancing my career and having a family would be hard. Making this choice was a radical exercise of my free will, and as adventurous and daring as it felt at the time, it was the making of my happiness.

As you reflect on your masterpiece in the making, what are the choices that await you? Are you single and contemplating married life? Are you a new mother, holding a baby in your arms? Are you a veteran mother who wants a fresh, revitalized vision of your vocation? You might choose whether to get engaged. You might choose to accept the Catholic Church's teaching on being open to life. You might choose to try to conceive. You might choose not to marry or have a child right now. You might choose to accept fully your unexpected pregnancy that has come about in dire circumstances or at an inconvenient time. You might choose to look into foster care or adoption. You might choose a name for your child. You might choose what job to hold and how many hours you will work outside the home. You might choose whether to grumble or accept it with serenity when your baby cries in the middle of the night. You might choose whether to shout in anger or to speak words of gentleness and kindness when your child misbehaves. You might choose whether to lie on the sofa and browse on your phone or get up and play a game with your child. You might look for a new way of praying for your children and teaching them the Faith. You might look for a way to be of support to your teenager, who seems distant these days.

When you make choices, you are not like a gerbil running through the maze of life. You have an intellect that can identify what is good, better, and best. You can exercise your freedom and choose what you think is the optimal option. When you do that, you are imitating God, who acts freely and always for the good. You are using a power that reflects the divine power of God, a privilege to have and an honor to use.

THE ART OF MOTHERHOOD: BUILD IT, AND THE DOME WILL FOLLOW

For many people, major life choices are a struggle. Often our struggles feel like weaknesses or deficiencies. When I am struggling, I often feel inadequate and ill-equipped and take it as a negative reflection of myself. But is that necessarily so? By taking our inspiration from artists and architects, we can instead see at least some of our struggles as part of our rich and fascinating human experience, an integral part of a successful life.

It is the year 1418 in Florence. Italy is not yet a nation, and out of the ceaseless barbaric invasions and plagues of the Middle Ages, Florence is emerging as a major city and economic center. Florence is cunning and capricious. It is self-governed and is replete with highly innovative, creative people whose family businesses and guilds are the heart of its economy.

Florence had a building boom in the 1300s, the likes of which it had not seen since it was a city of the ancient Roman Empire. As early as 1296, the foundation had been laid for a

Brunelleschi's Dome (Florence Duomo)

new basilica, Santa Maria del Fiore (Saint Mary of the Flowers), which would be the largest basilica in the known world. It would compete in size with the Hagia Sophia in Constantinople.

The problem is that now, in 1418, although the church walls have been built and priests say Mass in the sanctuary, the structure has no roof. To be more precise, it has no dome. A huge, thirty-foot scale model of the architect's plan is in the nave of the church along the southern wall. The model has a massive dome on top. Florentines have walked past this image for a hundred years, imagining the dome that has yet to be constructed successfully. But no one knows how to vault a dome this large. Attempts to do so have failed; the domes have collapsed. And so, without a dome, when it rains, it rains right inside the church. So the Florentines carry on, hoping that, one day, someone will come along and figure out the math to build the largest dome in the world.

What pluck! The Florentines had such gritty confidence that Florence herself would produce a genius who could complete the dome. It is a mark of this city's distinctive gutsiness that it built the cathedral and trusted that the dome would follow.

This can be how it feels to go out on a limb, saying yes to a proposal, saying no to a proposal, becoming open to having a child, adopting a child, taking a job with an infant at home, quitting or taking time off from a job you are invested in, going back to school while you have children at home, or making any number of major life choices. Your choice means the beginning of something that will take a long time to complete. You are in a half-built situation. That takes gumption. It takes nerve. Who knows how it will resolve? You may have a disaster on your hands. Then again, you may have made the most beautiful, ingenious life choice you'll ever make.

In fact, Florence did produce a man who was able to complete the dome. Filippo Brunelleschi, nicknamed "Pippo," had been apprenticed to a watchmaker and goldsmith when he was young, and he eventually set out on his own as a craftsman. His family home was not far from the unfinished cathedral, and he must have passed it daily his whole life long. When a competition to provide models for the dome was announced, Brunelleschi set to work and submitted a proposal. His was the only one that showed any promise, although he would not divulge the details of his plan. Despite intense controversy, the committee reluctantly chose him to build the dome. Having studied the domes and the architecture of ancient Rome and having reworked the math over and over, he finally came up with a solution that he believed would last. Forty years later, the dome was completed, making Filippo Brunelleschi the most famous architect in Europe. He created a circle of artists and shared with them his math, including his theories of how to use perspective, and the Renaissance was born.

What is your incomplete cathedral? What is your heart of hearts leading you toward? If today were Judgment Day and you were to stand before Christ, what would you have done with your life? Where do you, like Margaret Mary, sense Jesus wooing your soul, showing himself to you as the most beautiful, the wealthiest, the most powerful, the most perfect, and the most accomplished of all lovers?[18] While Margaret Mary found him in religious life, I can honestly say that it was in the thought of marrying Ron that I believed my full love for God and his created world, the fullness of my being, would be unleashed. In every case, each of us is called to give ourselves completely to the vocation that will bring about the full attainment of the highest good, which ultimately is God. May God bless you and the Holy Spirit guide you in constructing a masterpiece.

THE PRAYER OF MOTHERHOOD: SPIRITUAL EXERCISES FOR DISCERNMENT

Saint Ignatius of Loyola, a Spaniard of the 1500s, wrote a prayer manual called the *Spiritual Exercises*. In it, Ignatius gave a tool to help us make choices.[19] I hope it can serve you in making the important life choices that lie before you.

Ignatius' instruction is in how to read or analyze the interior forces and feelings that come when you are deliberating over a decision. When you make a choice, you are usually influenced by either a good feeling, prompting you to choose the thing, or a bad feeling, dissuading you from that thing. But how do you know whether those good and bad feelings are reliable?

Sometimes, you have a terrible feeling about what is actually a good thing. To use a nonspiritual example, you might be considering joining a softball team. You had been excited about it. But you suddenly have intense feelings of fear and dread. Where are these feelings coming from? Are they inspired by a true recognition that you do not have the adequate skill to play with this group? Or are they coming from insecurity, old memories of being laughed at by classmates in gym class, or resistance to something new? If they are coming from a realization of the truth, then you should heed them. If they are coming from insecurity and trauma, then you should detach from and overcome them. But how do you know the difference?

It is Ignatius' aim to help us understand those good and bad feelings. This is called *discernment*: identifying where those good and bad feelings are coming from.

First, Ignatius advises, ask yourself, "Is this experience a consolation or a desolation?" A *consolation* is an interior movement of the soul in which the soul is inflamed with the love of God, and when no created good can compete for our highest love. Consolation can also be any increase in faith, hope, and love. Alternatively, it can be an interior joy that draws us toward heavenly things and the salvation of our souls, giving them peace and making us feel at home in the presence of God.

A *desolation*, by contrast, is a darkness of the soul; an inner disturbance; a movement toward things earthly or base; a lack of confidence, or being without hope, without love; or a feeling of sadness, laziness, tepidness, or separation from God. Evil touches sharply, with noise and restlessness. If you are experiencing a desolation, Ignatius' advice is not to make any major decisions. Wait until the desolation is over before you act. This is because evil spirits can give us a desolation in order to sway us against a decision that God wants for us. In the meantime, increase your prayer and penance; do something good for someone else; take time to reflect inwardly, examining yourself and your relationship with God. The key virtue to have in a time of desolation is *patience*.

If you are experiencing a consolation, on the other hand, that is a good time to make decisions. The key virtue to have is *humility*: Remind yourself that this good thing that you are consoled about is coming from God — that, on your own strength and power, you could not have accomplished this positive situation — and ask God to help you protect and nurture the gift he has given you. As we make progress in the spiritual life, the good touches us lightly, gently, and sweetly, like a drop of water absorbed by a sponge.

Ignatius gives us a great tool in this ability to identify consolations and desolations. It can make all the difference when we are making a major life decision. Analyze your experience, and do your best to determine whether you are in consolation or desolation. It is not always obvious, and sometimes you are having neither. Sometimes you are just having a direct experience of positivity or negativity — for example, if I am fearful of a robber, that is just fear per se, not a desolation; if I have a positive experience of my husband sending me flowers, that is gratitude or pleasure, not a consolation. But seek to determine the inner workings of your heart and see what God is prompting you toward or away from. Listen to his voice and follow his guidance.

QUESTIONS FOR REFLECTION

1. Have you ever considered your freedom as a precious gift from God?
2. What is your reaction to Margaret Mary's story of the discovery of her freedom? Have you struggled to find your freedom? Or has it come more naturally to you?
3. How do Saint Gregory of Nyssa and Saint Thomas Aquinas impact your understanding or estimation of your freedom?
4. What is your story of dating, engagement, marriage, or discernment of a religious vocation? Have you ever exercised your freedom, or have you not discovered it yet? Are you ready to use your freedom with regard to motherhood? How will you do so?
5. What is your incomplete cathedral? What is the dome you are waiting for?
6. What do you think of Ignatius' keys to discernment? Right now, are you experiencing desolation or consolation? What do you think its purpose is? What do you think is God's path for you?

— 3 —

BEING HAPPY IN
THE FACE OF DEATH

As you design the masterpiece of your life, one of your main considerations must be your ultimate aim. What is the goal you are seeking? Ultimately, we seek happiness, but we fear expending energy on a project that might ultimately miss the mark. It is a sign of wisdom to make sure you have the right goal and the proper means to achieve it.

What does it take to be truly fulfilled? To be genuinely happy? Many philosophers as well as theologians have made the claim that love — both *eros*, which is the Greek word for passionate or erotic love, and *agape*, also Greek, meaning self-giving or sacrificial love — are key to happiness.[1] Exploring the ancient Greek philosopher Plato, the

early Christian martyrs Perpetua and Felicity, and the twenti-
eth-century Jewish thinker Viktor Frankl, we will see a variety
of accounts illustrating how a life of love can be a keystone to
the greatest thriving of the human person. Then we will see how
this insight finds its fulfillment in Christian love and applies to
motherhood. Next, in the Art of Motherhood, we will look at
the Sainte-Chappelle in Paris, one of the most beautiful Gothic
churches in the world. Then in the Prayer of Motherhood, we'll
explore Saint Thérèse's Little Way.

LOVE IS THE ANSWER

How do you become a wise woman who, at the end of your
life, will be able to look back and say, "I am happy. I made
the right choices"? Plato, a Greek philosopher who lived in
Athens in the fourth century B.C., wrote a magnificent work
that asks an outstanding question: How can we be happy in
the face of death?[2] Plato describes the final hours of the life
of Socrates, his mentor and friend. The scene is set in Socrates' prison cell, where he is going to be put to death on the
charge of having corrupted the youth of Athens. Plato gives
an account of Socrates' conversation with his friends while
they await his execution.

Rather than being despondent, frightened, and needing
encouragement from his friends, Socrates is portrayed as
calm and content. He upsets his friends by being so peaceful: "How could you possibly be so composed, while we are
so grieved?" they ask. Socrates makes a case to his weepy
friends as to why he so relaxed: A true philosopher should
be happy in the face of death. He reasons that, if a person
seeking wisdom has spent his whole life uniting his soul with
what transcends it, why should that person be upset when

the ultimate union finally comes?

The soul's pursuit of what is good Plato calls *eros*, or love. It is the passion of the soul reaching toward what it desires. Love, for Plato, is key to happiness. When we love the right things, we can become happy. Socrates reminds his friends that he has spent his whole life detached from earthly concerns of fame, reputation, wealth, and comfort. Instead, he has reached for, and pursued with singular attention, the divine. This is because the human being, Plato believes, is like an amphibian: humans have an immaterial soul "trapped in" a material body. So, humans are of two natures, one part spiritual and eternal, the other part physical and finite. The human being, unlike other earthly creatures, has an immortal soul that is oriented toward what is beyond it. The human soul belongs with the divine. Plato describes the divine as the Good, the Beautiful, and the Just. Human beings have an otherworldly soul in an earthly body. The philosopher is one who spends his or her whole life detached from fleeting, superficial goods, and seeking, pursuing, and loving what is eternal. That is why, in the face of death, Socrates is calm and resolute: He hopes his soul will finally be able to behold eternal reality in its fullness.

Socrates is saying to us: "What are you passionate about? What do you love? Are you attached to finite goods? Are you too bound up in the ephemeral values of the temporal world? Or have you set your sights on what lasts? Are you pursuing what really matters?" This message is suited for all kinds of mothers — even potential mothers. After all, mothers participate in the creation and rearing of human beings with immortal souls. Christian mothers in particular are "amphibian" in being oriented toward the eternal souls of their children while tending to their physical needs. Inevitably, the vocation of motherhood will lead us to various ways of creatively detaching ourselves from earthly values of wealth, public honor, and fame, and instead prioritizing what, in our maternal wisdom, we know has transcendent value.

ક્ષ

The story of Socrates' tranquility in the face of death is astonishingly similar to, and can be seen as an adumbration of, the various accounts of the martyrs of the early Church. One remarkable account is that of two mothers, Saints Perpetua and Felicity.[3] Perpetua was a young woman, twenty-two years of age, of noble birth and well educated, and the mother of an infant. When she was accused of being a Christian, her father begged her to renounce her faith. He said that he prized her above all her brothers and that she was the light of his life. Perpetua was unwilling to renounce her Christian faith and grieved that her father and her other family members could not rejoice with her in her impending martyrdom. She was put in a dungeon with other Christians. She was given the extraordinary grace of not worrying about her infant, and of not having pain from no longer nursing.

Felicity was a servant who was eight months pregnant. She, too, refused to renounce her faith and was put in the same prison. Pregnant women were not permitted to be publicly tortured. As a remarkable testimony of her faith, she prayed fervently for the early birth of her child so that she could be martyred with the others. The other prisoners joined her in passionate prayers to God for the delivery of the baby. Miraculously, their prayers were granted, and Felicity's sister took the child and raised her as her own daughter.

The soldier who guarded them was amazed at the holiness of the Christian prisoners, including the two young mothers. He allowed many visitors to come and be encouraged by them.

On the day of their martyrdom, Perpetua, Felicity, and their companions entered the amphitheater with joyous and brilliant countenances. Perpetua walked as though the bride of Christ, assured of being loved by God. Felicity rejoiced and regarded the blood she was about to shed as the second cleansing after childbirth, a second baptism. When Felicity was knocked down, Perpetua extended her hand and helped her up. Eventually the two women were destroyed by the beasts and the swords of the gladiators.

This account of the martyrdom of Perpetua and Felicity portrays the women willingly facing their death, in the pattern of Christ, who willingly gave himself up for us on the cross. His death was purposeful and efficacious. So too, the early Church martyrs saw their deaths as meritorious, and counted it a privilege to be among those who walked in the steps of Christ.

૪ð

If the question is how to be happy in the face of death, and Plato's answer is to love what is eternal, and Perpetua and Felicity's answer is to love Christ, another answer given by various philosophers and theologians is to *live a life of love*.

Viktor Frankl was a Jew who lived through World War II. A survivor of Dachau and Auschwitz, he was a direct witness to the Holocaust. He experienced firsthand Hitler's attempt to "cleanse" the German Empire of all those who did not have a place in his morbidly chilling "utopia."

The unspeakable horrors and human devastation of the World Wars brought clarity to many people regarding what actually matters. Many intellectuals wrote prolifically during and after both World Wars, searching for meaning as though for the first time. Some of these thinkers knew the traditional answers to the question of humanity's ultimate purpose: happiness, love, truth, and beatitude. Yet this crisis in human history threw into question all common answers, and these thinkers began to reconsider and rearticulate the discussion. What emerged by the end of World War II was a sober, penetrating, and beautiful testimony to the tenacity of the human spirit.

Viktor Frankl gives an extraordinary account of how he came to discover his answer to these fundamental questions, which is love. It deserves to be quoted fully:

> We stumbled on in the darkness, over big stones and through large puddles, along the one road leading from the camp. The accompanying guards kept shouting at us and driving us with the butts of their rifles. ... The man marching next to me whispered suddenly: "If our wives could see us now! I do hope they are better off in their camps and don't know what is happening to us."
>
> That brought thoughts of my own wife to mind. And as we stumbled on for miles, slipping on icy spots, supporting each other time and again, dragging one another up and onward, nothing was said, but we both knew: each of us was thinking of his wife. Occasionally I looked at the sky, where the stars were fading and the

pink light of the morning was beginning to spread behind a dark bank of clouds. But my mind clung to my
wife's image, imagining it with an uncanny acuteness. I
heard her answering me, saw her smile, her frank and
encouraging look. Real or not, her look was then more
luminous than the sun which was beginning to rise.

A thought transfixed me: for the first time in my
life I saw the truth as it is set into song by so many
poets, proclaimed as the final wisdom by so many
thinkers. The truth — that *love is the ultimate and the
highest goal to which Man can aspire.* Then I grasped
the meaning of the greatest secret that human poetry
and human thought and belief have to impart: *The
salvation of Man is through love and in love.* I understood how a man who has nothing left in this world
still may know bliss, be it only for a brief moment,
in the contemplation of his beloved. In a position of
utter desolation, when Man cannot express himself
in positive action, when his only achievement may
consist in enduring his sufferings in the right way —
an honorable way — in such a position Man can,
through loving contemplation of the image he carries
of his beloved, achieve fulfillment. For the first time
in my life I was able to understand the meaning of the
words, "The angels are lost in perpetual contemplation of an infinite glory."[4]

In this raw and moving passage, Frankl tells how he discovered anew the answer that he had not fully comprehended
until then: that "love is the ultimate and the highest goal to
which Man can aspire. ... The salvation of Man is through

love and in love."

Love, he urges, is the answer to the question of how to satisfy humanity's deepest aspirations. *Even in utter desolation, a person can be fulfilled.* That incredible conviction and rare insight emerged in Viktor Frankl amid the torturous conditions of the Nazi concentration camps. A person's fulfillment is not based on accomplishments, education or career, wealth or reputation, house or belongings, health, or even prospects for survival. No, even having lost every single worldly good, a human person still can be fulfilled "through loving contemplation of the image he carries of his beloved." How extraordinary! His love of his beloved leads Frankl to understand the meaning of the angels' love for God. Love in this present life and in the next; love temporal and eternal; love incarnate and infinite: This, for Frankl, is the greatest good of the human person.

John Paul II also witnessed World War II, and his response to the question of happiness in the face of death is similar: The human person is *made for love.* As a Polish priest, he chose to combat the evils of communism and fascism, not with weapons or war, but with metaphysics.[5] He poured his effort into articulating how human beings are made and what they need to thrive. His answer: Love is the fullest realization of the possibilities inherent in human persons.[6] Many vocations make this possible: religious life, single or married life, and the many possible career choices that one can take up as either a religious or a layperson. For John Paul II, motherhood is one of the ways a woman can achieve her greatest capacities.

John Paul II invokes a paradox: The human person cannot fully find himself or herself except through a sincere gift of self.[7] Being a person means striving toward self-realization, which, John Paul II boldly claims, can be achieved only through making oneself a gift to another. This is a great irony, since we usually imagine that self-realization means gaining or adding to what one has or can do. But John Paul II suggests that it is in *giving* oneself as a gift that one can find oneself. The human person "is called to exist 'for' others, to become a gift."[8] At its best, motherhood is an opportunity for women to make this gift of self, to exercise self-donation. In such a case, motherhood satisfies the deepest yearnings of the heart and helps us realize ourselves most fully. This is true of biological mothers, adoptive and foster mothers, stepmothers, grandmothers, and spiritual mothers of all kinds.

John Paul II goes on to reflect on biological motherhood: "Motherhood is the fruit of the marriage union of a man and woman … that brings about — on the woman's part — a special gift of self."[9] This kind of motherhood, he stresses, has an essential link to the sincere gift of self, since being open to conceiving a child and bringing him or her into the world constitutes a special moment in the mutual self-giving by the woman and the man.[10] "Although both of them together are parents of their child, *the woman's motherhood constitutes a special part in this shared parenthood,* and the most demanding part."[11] John Paul II goes on to say that motherhood involves a special communion with the mystery of life, a sharing in the great mystery of eternal generation.[12] It is thus one of the choicest ways a human being can find ultimate fulfillment.

We might also reflect on how this is true of women who choose to foster or adopt children. Such women open their hearts, lives, and homes to other human beings. Even in the absence of a hormonal and genetic bond, these women choose to give themselves as mothers. This is an extraordinary path, different from biological motherhood, but one that highlights the deliberate choice of entering into a personal communion of love. Adoption and foster parenting are especially beautiful ways of making a total and complete gift of self.

When they are fulfilled, according to John Paul II, human beings rise above the perversions of human behavior that the world witnessed in fascism and World War II. This is why family life and motherhood in particular are, for John Paul II, an answer to the worst evil humanity has ever seen; they are the antidote and healing of our world.

John Paul II's successor, Pope Benedict XVI, agrees with this point, and reflects that the love described by the ancient Greeks, *eros*, finds its ultimate meaning and fulfillment in the Christian notion of *agape*. "[Whereas *eros* is] an indeterminate, 'searching' love, [*agape*] moves beyond [a] selfish character. ... It seeks the good of the beloved: it becomes renunciation and it is ready, even willing, for sacrifice."[13] *Eros* is a searching love, whereas *agape* is a self-giving love. *Agape* is that personal love by which God chooses Israel and loves her — with a view to healing the whole human race.[14] God is love, *Agape*.

Benedict XVI takes up an important question: Are *eros* and *agape* fundamentally different? Are they opposed to each other? One might think that passionate, romantic love epitomized by two lovers is different from and even undermined by sacrificial, divine love. He quotes Friedrich Nietzsche as representative of this view, having said that "Christianity has poisoned *eros*."[15] But for Benedict XVI, *eros* and *agape* can never be completely separated.[16] Benedict XVI proposes that *eros* is rooted in the nature of every human being, and it finds its fulfillment in an exclusive and lifelong marriage oriented toward fruitfulness. He describes God in the Old Testament as revealing himself as loving Israel like a lover. Benedict asserts that in the best cases, *eros* develops into *agape*. Rather than being opposed to each other, these loves are compatible. Just as God loves us with a personal and elective love, reflected in the romantic love of a husband and a wife, this love is fully manifested in self-gift, as exemplified by Christ on the cross. The fully developed human love mirrors God, being both *eros* and *agape*. The Christian family thus becomes "an icon of the relationship between God and his people and vice versa."[17]

MOTHERHOOD AS A PROGRESSIVE LIFE CHOICE

As a woman discerning or living out family life, you have choices to make. How are you going to use your freedom? What do you think will make you truly happy?

Are you going to live for yourself? For dominance, legacy, or wealth? Are you going to live for a man-made goal or ideal? Are you going to live for political power? Or are you going to make the radical choice for a life of love, a life that is a gift for other people? This is a scary concept, because what if living for others does not pan out so well for *you*?

The answer of these philosophers and theologians to the question "What will make me happy?" is *love*, of which motherhood is an outstanding model. For single, married, divorced, or widowed women, motherhood in all its types can satisfy our deepest yearnings for lasting love and can be the crowning jewel of our lives. Motherhood is a special way of making oneself a gift, open to new life and participating in a unique way in the procreation of new human beings. It can be for many women an essential part of what makes them truly happy. It is not an antiquated, old-fashioned life choice. It is not "traditional" as opposed to forward-thinking. In the light of the World Wars and the deepest philosophical and theological reflection that ensued, motherhood is one of the most progressive, forward-thinking choices a woman in the twenty-first century can make.

Motherhood involves both *eros* and *agape*. It involves *eros* in the sense of satisfying our inner yearnings, which look different for each woman. Some women yearn for pregnancy; others for a baby in their arms. Some women desire to have a house brimming with children; others can't imagine becoming a mother, but have a distinct and even passionate desire for a spouse. Motherly instinct manifests itself differently from woman to woman, but it is often strong and even relentless.

The life of a mother is also decidedly marked by *agape*. It is constantly other-focused, constantly sacrificial in the best, Christian sense. One mother is torn open on the delivery table, shedding blood for the new little life that has been born. Another mother is holding her new child for the first time, after many long, arduous, expensive years working with adoption agencies. Another mother takes her new stepson out to a celebration dinner after the wedding, initiating the beginning of their mother-son relationship.

The loving life of a mother is exemplified by waking up in the night with a concerned heart for her crying child; rocking, feeding, wiping, caressing, nurturing, instructing, forgiving, laughing, holding for long minutes or hours a precious little human person in her lap. It is exemplified by racing her child to school; wiping throw-up off her daughter's face; staying up late to help her child with homework, skills, and projects. It is exemplified by supporting his friendships, athletics, and talents, and in her heart skipping a few beats when she hears of her child's first love.

The life of the mother of a teenager changes as that teenager develops autonomy. Motherhood for her now becomes forcing herself to remain quiet; choosing not to overcorrect; going to bed worried; wondering if she has taught well enough, loved well enough, lived well enough; delighting in this magnificent adult who came from her care; marveling at the teenager's good choice; wondering about all those other choices; being in awe of the teenager's interests and traits that did not come from her; feeling proud and small and left behind, all at the same time. Motherhood is a mix of paradoxes: giving so much away only to find oneself richer; gaining so much and yet watching it grow up and depart. Motherhood is an ache and a joy. It is frustration and delight.

Motherhood can be a Christian vocation, lived out as a life of love. It is a vocation whose paradigm is giving yourself to someone else who is lovable, and yet has done absolutely nothing to merit your love: "Greater love has no man than this, that a man lay down his life for his friends" (Jn 15:13). As a mother, you lay down your life daily for your child. Your child has not paid for it, won it, or worked for it. He has not behaved well enough for you to like him all the time, or even a lot of the time. And yet you choose to love him. You choose *him* over *yourself* — again and again and again. You take him to practices and appointments and playdates and outings instead of doing what you want. You cook this meal, you clean that shirt, you listen to that joke for the hundredth time; you watch his little one-man plays and help him learn to read; you burn in your guts when another child is rude to him. It is a life in which you offer to an undeserving soul your time, your body, your effort, your care, your heart. It leaves you immolated, rarefied, and purified of lesser concerns.

At its best, it is a singular life of love. It is worthy of your freedom and worth the leap. It is a cruciform life: a life in the shape of a cross. It is a way of losing one's life, only to find it anew (see Mt 16:25). It is a life that falls to the ground, bearing new life that will last for many generations (Jn 12:24). It is a way to be last, a "servant of all," which is how to become first in God's kingdom (Mk 9:35). If you give it your sincere effort and plunge it in daily baths of grace and prayer, it may not leave you successful in the way you had imagined in the worldly sense. But it will leave you satisfied in the spiritual sense, and prepared for the eve of life, when Christ lovingly looks you in the eye and, in hopeful anticipation, asks you about your life of love.

JUDGED ON LOVE

I was prompted to a life of love when I unexpectedly happened upon this quote by Saint John of the Cross: "In the eve of life, we will be judged on love." Judged on *love*? I questioned. I had always imagined that what will matter in the eve of life will be my accomplishments, all the more so if they are Christian ones. *Love?* I pondered. I imagined God judging me on how much I had loved him and others. What had I done by the grace of God that would elicit the words from Christ's lips: "Well done, my good and faithful servant. Well done, my beloved Kathryn"?

It was then that I began to view my marriage and children in a new way. I realized that I had been living for my own success. I wanted *my* degree. I wanted *my* career. I wanted *my* marriage. Even though my degree was in Christian education, even though my career in teaching would benefit others, even though my marriage was on a Christian foundation and I genuinely loved my husband — in all these cases, if I had to be honest, *it was all about me.* I wanted to be applauded by those around me; I wanted to have a good academic reputation; I wanted a marriage to satisfy my own heart's desires.

Reflecting more on this quote, I began to approach my husband differently. I tried to ask him more often about what he was thinking or feeling or going through, and not respond with something about my own experience. I challenged myself to talk with him without introducing myself into the conversation. I got to know him better, and this delighted me. I became downright tickled by the way he thinks, the little idiosyncrasies and quirks in his personality, and his way of doing things. He is so different from me! I had not known the extent of it until I stopped thinking of him in terms of what he can do for me, and instead, started thinking of him in his own right. I became almost intoxicated by how endearing he is in the humble and specific way he does things. I fell more in love with him and felt closer to him as I got to know him in this new way. This notion of living for love also assisted me a great deal in "letting him be him" with our kids. Rather than always pushing him to do things my way in how we raised them, I made room for his very different and, I discovered, wonderful ways of relating to them.

Without any doubt, my new desire to live for love transformed my motherhood. It cultivated within me a readiness to *enjoy* the selflessness and other-focused lifestyle that motherhood is. It helped me to be more open to motherhood's demands which I had feared would result in my not getting what I needed. I embraced living for others, I overcame my hesitations, and I decided to go for it full-throttle. I decided to take the gamble that not focusing on getting what I needed, and focusing on the needs of others, might result in my getting what I needed after all.

With the help of this vision of living a life of love, I dove into my vocation of marriage and motherhood. The result has been exactly what Viktor Frankl, John Paul II, and Benedict XVI have said: I have become truly happy. I am fulfilled. I do not have doubts about my life, my worth, my significance, or my vocation. When things do not go as I had hoped, I have an otherworldly notion that, if I am living for love and making of myself a gift, it will all turn out well. Perhaps this is how nuns, overseas missionaries, and other radical Christians feel: Their success is truly not of the world, and they are fulfilled because they trust that their vocation will result in union with God and fruits that will please him. That is the life of being a wife and mother for me: I have chosen a life of love and self-donation because I believe that this is how we are designed to live, that no human being can be happy without love, and that it is upon love that God judges us. Through this life, I find a deepening of my faith, and I pray that God will be pleased with my humble efforts. For me, Catholic marriage and motherhood is how to be happy in the face of death. If I were to die today, I would die a happy woman. Against all odds, I have found a path to true happiness, and it is one I hope you, too, will discover.

THE ART OF MOTHERHOOD:
THE SAINTE-CHAPELLE

When a person makes that rare choice, the conscious decision to live for love and make her whole life a gift to others, that person becomes a jewel. Her life is like a precious jewel

Sainte-Chappelle, Île de la Cité, Paris, France

box, radiant with beauty. It calls to mind perhaps the most beautiful church of all time, the Sainte-Chapelle in Paris. The "Holy Chapel" is a not a grand cathedral or basilica like Chartres or Saint Peter's. It is a small chapel, built by Saint Louis IX in 1248 to house relics of the passion, including Christ's crown of thorns. With slender pillars leading up to pointed arches serving as the "bones" of the walls and ceiling, all the space in between is dedicated to massive stained-glass windows; 1,113 windows make up the walls. When I first entered the chapel, I lost my breath, as I had never seen a church made almost entirely out of glass. The shimmering colors are like jewels, and the pillars glisten with gold. It is, in my view, distinctly feminine, having a lightness and delicacy that most churches lack. The church is reminiscent of heaven.

This is an image of the life of a mother who chooses to make herself a gift. She is a depiction of heaven on earth. She helps others see beyond this world, a shining example of the transcendent. The chapel is one of the finest examples of Gothic architecture, displaying a sense of weightlessness and a thrust upward toward heaven. So, too, the life of a mother can be a life that shows a supernatural quality and a life aimed at eternity.

Built to house a treasure, the housing itself is a treasure. So too, a biological, adoptive, step, or spiritual mother houses a baby, maybe in her womb, maybe cradled in her arms, maybe welcomed into her home, always in her heart. She thereby becomes a treasure, making her life a gift and cherishing the gift of her child.

How does Sainte-Chapelle inspire you to make a treasure out of your life? How might you be transformed into a temple of God housing rare treasures? Are you called to the sacred life of motherhood — a life of love whereby, making yourself a gift to your husband, your gift multiplies and comes back to bless you with the gifts of your children?

THE PRAYER OF MOTHERHOOD: THÉRÈSE'S LITTLE WAY

Saint Thérèse of Lisieux is a spiritual master whose main teaching is love. A Doctor of the Church, Saint Thérèse is well known for her Little Way, which is especially helpful for those who are trying to live lives pleasing to God, and whose lives involve at least some aspect of self-denial. Some people can live "big" lives pleasing to God by being brilliant or talented or powerful or famous. Billy Graham and the pope — we hope and pray — are pleasing to God. But what about deliberately choosing small things, even occasionally, as a path to God? Could it be that the little events of our lives might be occasions for pleasing God uniquely? Could this be part of the essence of the Gospel? Thérèse's Little Way can equip mothers to make every moment of motherhood an act of love that is hugely pleasing to God and a path to union with him.

Thérèse's Little Way begins with her recounting how deeply irritating some of the sisters in her convent were. Some of them fidgeted. Some of them left things out of place. Some of them made irritating noises. One of her superiors regularly spent an hour at a time criticizing Thérèse. Another of her superiors mocked her in front of the whole community for overlooking a cobweb when she herself had been tasked with dusting. On one occasion, a superior reprimanded Thérèse for chipping a vase. Although she had not caused the break, Thérèse chose to accept the scolding and asked for forgiveness. This event stood out as one of the hardest experiences for Thérèse, who desperately desired to defend herself. Her choice to forgo self-defense was her Little Way of choosing spiritual martyrdom and drawing closer to Christ.

Thérèse explains how she came to this Little Way. She had always desired to be a great saint, but felt as "far removed from them as a grain of sand trampled under-foot by the passer-by is from a mountain whose summit is lost in the clouds."[18] Instead of being discouraged, she set out to find a way to God that was very short, very straight, and entirely new.

She found this way in Scripture: "Whoever is simple, let him turn in here!" (Prv 9:4) and "You shall be carried upon her hip, and fondled upon her knees. As one whom his mother comforts, so will I comfort you" (Is 66:12–13).[19] She saw Jesus as the one who, like a tender mother, would be content with her little child drawing close. If Thérèse could be as close to Jesus as a young child in her mother's arms, Jesus would bring her to heaven.

How could Thérèse draw close to Christ? She says that she is too little for great and magnificent martyrdom, like Perpetua's and Felicity's. Rather, in her simplicity, Thérèse found martyrdom — a great spiritual event — in the smallest of things.[20] She learned to love the annoying people in her life and love Christ by embracing the things that offended or hurt her.

Thérèse had a least favorite sister in the convent, but she approached interactions with her as opportunities for sanctity: Every time she saw the sister, Thérèse prayed for her and did little acts of charity for her. One day, the annoying sister said, "*Soeur* Thérèse, what is it that attracts you to me so strongly? I never meet you without being welcomed by your gracious smile."[21] Thérèse had become a master of love.

The Little Way of Saint Thérèse consists in accepting, with the motivation of love, the small frustrations of life. In her autobiography she writes:

> On another occasion when I was engaged in the laundry, the Sister opposite to me, who was washing handkerchiefs, kept splashing me continually with dirty water. My first impulse was to draw back and wipe my face in order to show her that I wanted her to be more careful. The next moment, however, ... I carefully refrained from betraying any annoyance. On the contrary, I made such efforts to welcome the shower of dirty water that at the end of half an hour

I had taken quite a fancy to the novel kind of asper-
sion and resolved to return as often as possible to the
place where such treasures were freely bestowed.[22]

Thérèse's ambition was to overcome her instinctual reactions,
or her "nature,"[23] as she sometimes called it, to accept small
discomforts and annoyances.

An even more intense martyrdom for Thérèse was a
dark night of the soul, in which she experienced profound
aridity and a feeling of horrible heaviness and dreariness.
Grave physical suffering began with bleeding in the mouth,
a sign of the tuberculosis from which she eventually died. In
the smallest to the biggest difficulties, Thérèse aspired not
to react according to her nature, but to show no negative
reaction at all (and sometimes even a positive one). Some of
the sisters in her convent accused her of faking her illness,
since she showed so little discomfort, although she had pain
so severe that she said, without faith, she would have eagerly
taken her life. She said, "To soar above all natural sentiment
brings the deepest peace, nor is there any joy equal to that
which is felt by the truly poor in spirit."[24] This Little Way was
her great martyrdom.

Thérèse's Little Way is well suited to motherhood, not
only because it is inspired by seeing Christ reaching out to us
with motherly love, but also because motherhood is a vocation
based on loving magnificently and generously through many
little tasks. I consider myself in the school of Saint Thérèse,
always at the bottom level of instruction. Just this morning, I
reached for the scissors where they ought to have been in the
kitchen, only to find them missing — one of my children had
taken them to cut out paper dolls and snowflakes. I had to

stop for a moment and choose: How should I respond? Can I respond lovingly? Many times I fall short, but each and every moment of motherhood is an opportunity to "soar above all natural sentiment."

Some events in the life of a mother are more serious and have a lasting impact. My friend Tamara, mother of eight, found out she was expecting twins. Her unexpected pregnancy was a true martyrdom — the opportunity to yield to God and follow Thérèse's Little Way. She learned to accept each day of bloated feet, each hour of indigestion, each fear that came with their financial distress as a chance not to complain, not to panic, not to remain in self-pity or anger, but rather to yield, problem-solve, and trust in God. Over tea at a friend's house, I asked her, "How do you do it?" She replied, "I know that God's greatest desire of me is to love him and trust in him as his little child."

Another friend, Silvia, experienced infertility for many years. In her long wait for a child, knowing that she might never conceive, she struggled with fear, anxiety, and shame. She found, however, in Saint Thérèse's Little Way a new approach that gave her relief. When I asked her how she responded to her intense feelings of distress, she said, "God gives each person crosses, and it is only by embracing those crosses that we find our own path to heaven." Whenever her dreaded period came, she imagined it as a spiritual martyrdom. She sought to overcome her natural tendencies, and, as the martyrs who have gone before her trusted God in their loss and shame, so, too, Silvia chose this private but intense suffering as her path to the arms of Christ.

This kind of approach requires incredible, supernatural effort to overcome our natural tendencies, but it can make potential and actual mothers great saints. It is through such choices that we can draw close to the arms of Jesus. He is there, waiting for us to crawl onto his lap. This is a way to love him. By choosing not to indulge in our natural reaction, but instead to be peaceful, kind, and loving, we accept the full spiritual martyrdom available to us in that moment. As spiritual "martyrs," we are Christ's beloved, showing our sincere desire to please him. The genius of Saint Thérèse is to give love purely and completely to God in the small, insignificant moments of our lives. As Saint Teresa of Calcutta, so deeply influenced by Saint Thérèse, summed it up: "I am a little pencil in the hand of a writing God, who is sending a love letter to the world." Each mother can use the little trials that are built into the very fabric of her vocation as a lifelong series of opportunities to write the world a love letter about God's love.

QUESTIONS FOR REFLECTION

1. What do you think it will take for you to be happy in the face of death?

2. Do you think that Plato's answer — to love eternal truths — is compatible with Viktor Frankl's, John Paul II's, and Benedict XVI's answers? How are their answers similar, and how are they different?

3. Where does love fall as a priority in your life?

4. When you hear Saint John of the Cross's quote, "In the eve of life, we will be judged on love," what thoughts or feelings arise in your heart?

5. Do you love people by listening to them, or do you often insert yourself into people's accounts of their own experiences?

6. How can your vocation make a treasure out of your life? Does that goal compel you? Describe your reaction to the reflection on Sainte-Chapelle.

7. Have you already learned about Saint Thérèse's Little Way? How successful are you at practicing it? Does it encourage you to overcome your first impulses when they are negative and to find a path to God in little acts?

their churches, or the
To come to g
as a happy wo
we are goin
ply it to
mot

— 4 —

HOW TO FLOURISH

Even after deciding to live for love and make your life a gift, you still have significant practical questions to consider. "What about my career?" you might ask yourself. My income? My chance to do something great with my life? Are marriage and motherhood fulfilling enough? Will they satisfy all of who I am? Though we should not neglect the life to come, we still ought to give this current life its proper due. For many women, true happiness involves not only marriage and motherhood, but actualizing other aspects of who they are, which may include earning an income, supporting or helping to support their families, and using their talents for the benefit of society. They are women with educations, marketable skills, and desires to help their communities, world around them.

eater clarity about what it means to flourish
man and a mother in the twenty-first century,
g to look at Aristotle's notion of flourishing and ap-
women today. We will also look at three modern-day
er saints and reflect on a variety of ways in which they
ngaged with work outside the home. We will then consider
five great options for how women today can design their lives
and flourish: full-time work outside the home, part-time work
outside the home, reprieves from work outside the home, a career later in life, and staying at home with children. In the Art
of Motherhood, we will look at Michelangelo's Sistine Chapel
and the significance of Eve's appearance at its center. We will
end with a tool for your toolbox, using Saint Catherine of Siena's view of self-knowledge as a means to help you discern the
will of God for your unique life.

ARISTOTLE ON FLOURISHING

Whereas Plato's answer about how to be happy in the face
of death pointed to eternal truths that exist beyond the visible world, his student Aristotle gave a somewhat different
answer. Aristotle's concept of happiness, or *eudaimonia*, is
often understood in terms of flourishing. Flourishing, for
Aristotle, is a stable state of being able to act with intellectual
and moral virtue over the course of one's whole life: "He will
do and contemplate what is excellent, and he will bear the
chances of life most nobly."[1] Aristotle emphasizes virtue in
our day-to-day choices as the key to achieving *eudaimonia*.

Aristotle's view of flourishing is easiest to understand
when he talks about things in nature. He describes them in
terms of actuality and potentiality: An acorn has the potential

to become an oak tree; a tadpole has the potential to become a mature frog. A potentiality, for Aristotle, is real, even though it does not exist yet as an actuality. The acorn does not and never will have the potential to become a frog or to speak Spanish, but it does have the potential to become a tree. An acorn has a real potential that differs from the potentiality of a tadpole or of a human being. Things thrive in nature when their potentialities become actualized, that is, when things grow and achieve their end or goal, such as when the tadpole becomes a mature frog. For Aristotle, the natural world is brimming with potentiality and yearns to become actualized. Nature is a dynamic order driven to thrive.

Aristotle says that human flourishing can be learned through teaching, training, and habit. "The things we have to learn before we can do, we learn by doing."[2] That is, if you don't yet have a certain ability or virtue, you begin acting according to that virtue it will grow in you, just as those who cannot yet lift heavy weights should start lifting weights as heavy as possible so that they will develop greater strength over time. Aristotle's notion of human flourishing, then, involves developing moral strengths, abilities, and knowledge that one does not innately have. Aristotle adds that we can also acquire skills and expertise pertaining to sciences and crafts that contribute to the world around us: He uses as examples medicine, building, and finance. All of this can help one to thrive, not in an otherworldly sense, but in a this-worldly sense.

Part of nature's thriving, Aristotle claims, pertains to motherhood: He describes generation and reproduction as a living thing's way of partaking "in the eternal and divine."[3] He says that even as living things die, their species persists through the act of generation. It is good, Aristotle believes, for a thing to be able to produce its like. Beings that reproduce assist their species to endure over time, and this is a vital part of the flourishing of nature.

ℰ

Applying these ideas to motherhood, we can understand that for some twenty-first century mothers, motherhood in itself is a way to thrive. For some, that means bringing new life into the world; for others, it means adopting a child; for most, it means raising children to be competent, happy adults. For many twenty-first century mothers, flourishing will mean not only having children, but also developing capacities, cultivating talents, learning skills, growing in moral excellence, and acquiring knowledge. For many twenty-first century women, this will mean getting an education and working outside the home, using their skills, insight, and talents. For them, being made in the image and likeness of God (Gn 1:26) means to be creative, both in and outside the home.[4]

This is a new era for humanity, one in which women have unprecedented opportunities for work, income, self-realization, and the chance to make contributions to a healthy society. I believe that our culture needs women in all our industries and on all levels of leadership and service in order to bring what is distinctly feminine to our world. This is also a time in which the evil of prejudice is being overcome, and women are experiencing more and more equitable treatment. I encourage women, and especially Catholic women, to foster this positive development as they are compelled by material needs and by the desire to share their skills and talents. I also encourage mothers of all kinds to find their way to prioritize motherhood in their lives. Our society will not truly be healed and justice will not genuinely be manifest until mothers are appreciated for their essential role in our world.

As you are discerning your twenty-first century life and pondering how you should flourish, I would like to offer you the stories of three modern mothers who are canonized saints. Perhaps their stories will help guide you as you imagine your life and artistically design your future, blending work in and outside of the home. Each one of them is different, and their holiness is manifested in ways specific to them as unique persons.

In what direction is God calling you? How are you called to serve him and make the Church and the world better places? Let these women befriend you and help you find your way.

Gianna

Dr. Gianna Beretta was a full-time pediatrician, family doctor, and surgeon who also served the elderly and the poor. She was a well-educated woman whose siblings included two engineers, four physicians, a pharmacist, and a concert pianist. One of her brothers was a priest, and one of her sisters was a nun. She was also a vibrant Catholic, whose parents were Third Order Franciscans. Gianna attended Mass and said the Rosary every day and loved skiing, theater, and dancing.

She considered being an overseas missionary, but she determined instead that she had a vocation to family. In her mid-thirties, she met Pietro Molla, who fell in love with this vivacious and outgoing woman: "I had fallen in love, but I did not find words to express my feelings. Thank God … I found a complement in this woman who was more open, more effusive than myself."[5]

Pietro and Gianna married and had three children. Then Gianna had two miscarriages. During these years, Dr. Gianna Beretta Molla maintained a full-time practice as they raised their family. Gianna's life was a juggling act, one that many twentieth and twenty-first century women are familiar with: home life, career, and serving in Catholic Action, which aimed at promoting Catholic influence on society, and in the Society of Saint Vincent de Paul, which served the poor. Gianna also took time for her extended family. She was a busy woman, always on the run. She emphasized to her husband, however, the importance of taking time to rest, play, and live life joyfully. And so they had season tickets to the theater and took Sundays off to spend together as a family.

Then the Mollas had a sixth pregnancy, which, by the grace of God, became the occasion for Gianna's greatest display of sanctity. Doctors discovered a tumor inside her uterus, alongside the baby. Gianna begged the doctors to save the life of her child, even if it meant risking her own. This meant rejecting both abortion and a hysterectomy, either of which would have saved her life. This decision became widely known among the community.

The doctors performed surgery to remove the tumor, and Gianna recovered and went back to work in her medical practice. She worked and raised her family during the remaining months of pregnancy. Even though there were complications, she carried the baby full-term as a full-time working mom.

In an incredibly sad turn of events, Gianna died a week after she gave birth to the child, from a complication due to the surgery she had chosen. She became widely known as the woman who was willing to die so that her child might live. Forty-four years later, Gianna's husband and three living children attended her canonization in St. Peter's Square — the first canonization of a wife attended by her husband.[6] Gianna is the patron saint of mothers, physicians, and unborn children.

Zélie

Zélie Guérin (1831–77) was a Frenchwoman canonized in 2008 with her husband, Louis Martin, the first married couple to be canonized together. They had nine children, five of whom lived to be adults, all of whom became Catholic nuns. The youngest was Saint Thérèse of Lisieux, "the greatest saint of modern times" according to Pope Saint Pius X.

Like Gianna, Zélie was a professional. At the age of nineteen, she quit her job in a lace factory and began her own business making Alençon lace, an exquisite, intricate form of lace very popular at the time. At the age of twenty-six, she married thirty-five-year-old Louis Martin, who made his living as a watchmaker. Zélie's business was so successful that twelve years into their marriage, Louis sold his shop and went into partnership with her. Zélie had nine employees who helped her sew the lace, and Louis took care of the books and sales, selling their lace locally and in Paris.

Zélie ran her business while having her many children. She cared for her children throughout the day with the help of a nanny who lived on the premises. She woke early and stayed up late so she could do her work when the children were sleeping. She had many sleep-deprived nights and often felt completely over-extended.

But it was important to Zélie to prioritize having a happy, joyful home. She herself had a stern mother who had often neglected her. Zélie chose the opposite approach, and her children described her as happy, doting, always hugging them and smiling at them. The house was joyful when the little ones were young, with many simple games and songs.

Unlike Gianna, Zélie was not one to take days off for leisure. Sundays were devoted to God, and the family spent many hours in Mass and adoration (sometimes attending two or three Masses each Sunday). Zélie and Louis did not socialize by going out on dates or being a part of the society. Their priorities were being home, serving God and their family, and successfully running their business.

Zélie and Louis chose not to earn money on the Sabbath. The lace business was closed for business on Sundays, even though on Sunday the markets were full of shoppers. They also treated their employees with great fairness and love. They didn't cut corners, nor did they seek wealth at any cost. Still, their business prospered, and they amassed a small fortune.

Zélie loved her work. She wrote: "To tell you the truth, I am not really happy unless I am seated at my window assembling my lace pieces." The Martin children suffered at times from their mother's dedication to her career. One of her daughters came to despise her mother's work, as it took so much time away from her (though this did not stop her from becoming a joyful person and a nun). Zélie continued to work in order to secure her daughters' financial security.

Zélie Guérin Martin's sanctity was not in being a mystic, a missionary, or a martyr. It was in giving her life to God through the vocation to family. She gave everything — all her time, all her energy, all her love. She did this as a full-time owner of a business. She knew the importance of having help, including the help of her husband and a live-in nanny. Amid the real-life joys and struggles of raising a family, she is a model wife, mother, and working professional.

Elizabeth

Elizabeth Ann Seton (1774–1821), the first American-born saint to be canonized, was a wife, a mother, and a professional. Elizabeth was born an Episcopalian. She and her husband lived in New York City and had five children, but when the youngest was an infant, her husband died in bankruptcy, and Elizabeth was left widowed and poor. She and one of her daughters had spent time in Italy at the end of her husband's life, and there she discovered a desire to become Catholic. She returned to the United States and had to rebuild her life — both financially as the sole breadwinner, and as a convert to Catholicism.

First, Elizabeth got a job. Living again in New York City, she opened a boarding house for boys, a common thing for a woman at that time to do. This job did not last, because the parents of the boys had strong anti-Catholic sentiments. The parents removed their boys from her boarding house, to the Seton family's detriment.

Next, two years after her conversion, when her oldest child was thirteen and her youngest was six, Elizabeth was invited by several priests to move to Baltimore, Maryland, to open a school for girls. Other women from other states came to join her work, and her school became the first free school for Catholic girls. This school became the beginning of the parochial school system in the United States.

The women soon moved to Emmitsburg, Maryland, where they formally began a religious order, the Sisters of Charity of St. Joseph's, in 1809 — all of this while Elizabeth still had five children at home. Elizabeth's sanctity lay in her courage to become Catholic; to raise and educate her children in the face of financial, religious, and cultural challenges; and even to become a spiritual mother and pave the way for the education of countless children. She was a brave woman and mother, and many people have benefited from her contribution to the Church.

જી

These women show a diversity of ways to raise a family and engage with work outside the home. Elizabeth worked out of financial need; Zélie could afford a nanny for her children. Elizabeth worked what would today be considered part-time when she ran a boarding house. Gianna and Zélie essentially worked full-time while raising small children, as did Elizabeth when running her schools.

Most mother saints throughout the ages, including ancient and medieval mothers — from Mary of Nazareth, to Monica, to Rita — were mainly concerned with raising their children as long as their children lived at home. And yet, who is to say that Mary did not sell woven fabrics, home-made food, or home-grown vegetables to locals? We know that Saint Monica served her church and the faithful once Saint Augustine was grown. Saint Rita may have helped her husband in supporting their family for the eighteen years of their marriage.

In short, there is precedent for women and mothers who are saints and whose lives were successful in the eyes of God to work, to earn a living, and to contribute to the world around them as they are so called. In our current world and economy, there is no reason to think that a woman can express her gifts and talents only through family life. On the other hand, it can be a bold, beautiful, creative choice to choose family life over more lucrative options. Some women find extraordinary joy in homemaking and raising children, and the world is a better place for every happy home. Additionally, for some women, choosing against work outside the home is a noble, sanctified choice. What is your calling? If you don't know yet, for whatever reason, spend some time thinking and praying about what you would like and what you would be open to. Let the Holy Spirit guide you to imagine how best you can serve God and the world.

CREATIVITY IN AND OUTSIDE THE HOME: FIVE OPTIONS

Women in the twenty-first century have the chance to weave motherhood into the other strands of their lives. This includes work "outside the home" (in the sense of paid work, whether at another location or remotely) in order to support themselves, express their talents, meet their needs, or build up the Church and the world, and thus to cultivate a flourishing life. This can be full-time work; full-time work except for periods of staying home with young children; part-time work; or a career developed later in life. Alternatively, and just as creatively, women can choose to stay at home with their children and express their talents and build up the Church and the world through motherhood. While one woman who chooses to stay at home with her children wishes for nothing else, another, pressured to pursue a career or earn an income, makes the boldest, bravest choice she can in choosing to stay home with her children. Whichever of these general categories a woman chooses is entirely hers creatively to determine. We will take a closer look at all five categories to help you discern how you are called to weave motherhood and your career, if you so choose, into your successful, twenty-first century life.

I. Full-Time

Mothers who choose full-time work outside the home may have specific callings from God, exceptional professional opportunities, the need to earn a living to support their families, or some combination thereof, each of which requires full-time work with the exception of maternity leave.

Many women in this category find fulfillment in their work as well as in their families. As working professionals who are also mothers, they can flourish. And our society needs them: Women constitute 47 percent of our country's workforce.[7] Though there is a cultural expectation that families have two incomes, it is strangely still the case that many women who have small children and work forty hours or more outside the home sometimes feel out of place. They have to go against the grain. They sometimes feel resistance from family and friends who think they should spend less time at work and more time with their children. They tend to rely on supportive husbands or other family members, as well as nannies, day care, and babysitters. With such help, they are glad that they can make the contribution to which they feel called and can flourish all the same. We would all do well to befriend women of this category and support them in their decisions. Our society will not be healthy until this group of women is a thriving, integrated part of our churches and our world.

II. Full-Time with Exceptions

Many mothers work full-time with exceptions. Having a career, taking time off when children are young, and then returning to full-time work may be the most popular option. Schoolteachers, nurses, and many professionals whose industry allows for taking a break and then jumping back in enjoy this possibility. Some mothers stop working outside the home when they have their first child and cannot imagine returning to work. But when their youngest goes to kindergarten, many of them consider the possibility of going back to work. Some need the income, others the fulfillment of doing something they once enjoyed and were good at and trained for, and others want both.

Countless mothers have taken this path for as long as women have been teachers and nurses and have held other jobs that allowed for a multiyear break. Our society needs these women: the schools, offices, medical groups, and businesses that employ them when they return to work after a several-year hiatus will tell you how valuable they are. May we always appreciate them and support them for the full range of creativity they bring to our culture and its families.

III. Part-Time Working Mothers

Mothers who work part-time out of the home or for pay are in good company: 64 percent of part-time workers are women, compared with 43 percent of full-time workers, meaning that more women prefer to work part-time than full-time. This data is compatible with the fact that two-thirds of mothers of children under eighteen prefer to stay home rather than work.[8] So, working part-time is a good compromise for many women. Another option many women choose is to work from home, whether part-time or full-time. Online shops, freelancing, virtual organizations, and businesses of all kinds allow moms to work at home. They steal hours when their children are asleep or when their husbands can give them some time; or if they can, they even work with their children around them.

Mothers may work virtually or part-time for any number of reasons. In addition to having children at home, some of them need the income. Others work part-time as a compromise, not working full-time, as they would otherwise want to. Still others work part-time for a sense of fulfillment beyond homemaking and child-rearing, but not out of obligation. One advantage of working part-time is that it allows women to continue using skills that could be employable down the road.

IV. Stay-at-Home Mothers

Two-thirds of women with children under eighteen years old prefer to stay home. For these women, their primary way of flourishing is through the home. Their talents, creativity, and love are mainly fulfilled in their family lives. This category is incredibly diverse. Some stay-at-home mothers want nothing more than to be able to stay home with their children. Others are trained in a career they love and are good at, and staying home is a sacrifice they make because they desire that bond with their children which is forged under the specific circumstances of being at home full-time. Some stay-at-home mothers cherish being home, and some of them are wonderful homemakers; others love their children but are not born with the talent of keeping a house. Some are wonderful cooks; others cannot boil an egg. Some are perpetual cleaners; others hire maids. Some of them have one child; others have a dozen. Some of them have children who are relatively easy to raise; others have special-needs children and pour themselves into caring for these beautiful people. Some of them are so wealthy that they have no need to earn an income; others make huge financial sacrifices to be home with their children. Staying at home is one decision that can be made for a multiplicity of reasons, can look countless different ways, and means something different from one woman to the next.

V. Careers Later in Life

Speaking as an older mother, I have been truly surprised by how many stay-at-home moms I have met who wanted or needed a career later in life. It really helps all women, even women who want to stay home with their children, to have an education and an employable skill, in case the need or desire to work or to be involved in a professional endeavor outside the home emerges later in life.

Some stay-at-home mothers are trained in careers and leave them to raise their families, but then find themselves re-engaged in careers, businesses, or nonprofits later in life. One mother goes back to work or starts a new chapter of her life as a working woman because of financial need. Another has stayed home for years, but then is asked to be on a board and serve in her trained capacity, which she does for free but finds fulfilling. Yet another is ready on a personal level to get back to her career, and her children appreciate her as a working woman. Still another was a devoted stay-at-home mom, but makes an unexpected career out of something she became good at — cooking, designing school rooms or children's rooms, or homeschooling. I find a constant source of inspiration in the richly diverse ways in which women uniquely weave motherhood and professional work into their lives.

I will be transparent here and tell you that I am deliberate with my own children, instructing them to make sure they are employable on the level on which they feel called to live. They may choose not to seek employment either for a season or for their whole adult lives, and I would be completely delighted with their being in any of the above categories. But I do not want my children to be vulnerable — suddenly widowed or divorced or suffering some financial upset — and not have a clear way forward. It may be hard to start a career late in life, but having the education for it is a huge, critical step toward security.

కా

How do we flourish as mothers? Having children can leave us tired out of our minds, foggy-headed, and stammering when proper sentences fail us. We can wonder whether the rat race of out-of-the-home work and in-the-home work is making our lives *flourish far less.* "Is anything getting done well? Are all my projects unfinished with not-so-good prospects for completion anytime soon? Am I giving my children enough attention? How is their spiritual formation? Social development? Are they reading good books? When was the last time I made a meal with fresh vegetables? Oh, shoot! I forgot to take my six-year-old to soccer practice today. I wonder how upset he will be." The life of a mother can be a long stream of consciousness of worries, frets, reminders, hopes not yet realized, and dreams not yet fulfilled. On any given day, it does not necessarily feel like flourishing.

But flourishing consists in being fecund and self-diffusive. As we have seen, Aristotle believes that the human person cannot be happy until she has achieved her potential and become all she can be. Flourishing means giving yourself — whether in childbearing, in rearing children, in your career, in support of your church or some organization that is important to you. It means making the biggest, boldest choice you can make for love, in and outside the home. Even if flourishing leaves you worn out, depleted, and not so great in today's appearance and performance, flourishing is to give yourself to others — to take yourself out of the center of your universe and to put there instead other precious, invaluable human beings.

Motherhood can be an essential part of your successful, twenty-first-century life. Motherhood is not a threat. If you have a vocation to family, then motherhood is a part of the perfect whole. It's a choice you bravely make. In making the choice to see your own motherhood as a treasure rather than a liability, you bring health to a culture. Our society is sick because it diminishes one of its life sources: motherhood. By choosing motherhood along with your education, career, and personal development, you are showing through the testimony of your life that maternal love is important for our culture, and we cannot survive without it. You can be a card-carrying mom, no matter what other titles you hold.

What is God's path for you? He has a special plan just for you. "I know the plans I have for you, says the LORD, plans for welfare and not for evil, to give you a future and a hope" (Jer 29:11). Become an artist. Don't just do what the professionals or family members or other role models in your life expect of you. Design your life *your way*. As you use your creativity, you will probably need help from other people. Most of all, you will need the inspiration of the Holy Spirit. Let him guide you. If your career is pleasing to God, you will know it, because he will reassure you. Do you want to do something really great with your life? I suggest seeing motherhood as central to that great achievement, and yet finding your unique way of incorporating other kinds of work and accomplishment into your life, if you feel inspired or required to do so. Can you do something really great with your life and still be a mother? Yes, you can.

How does this discussion about careers strike you? Where do these considerations leave you in regard to the compatibility of professional life and family life? Are you more motivated to try to maintain your professional career? Or, as you have been reflecting throughout these chapters on the importance and beauty of motherhood, is the appeal of your out-of-the-home career losing its grip on you? My personal view is that it is a gorgeous, scintillating reality that that decision is *between you and God*. Please allow the reflections in this book to serve only to elevate your awareness of your freedom to follow God's specific call for your life. If there is one message that I am trying to send, however, it is that motherhood matters. Remember how gloriously important it is. Whatever time you are with your child or children, whether that is 24/7 or once you are off work, make it count. See it for all it is worth and take full advantage of the opportunity it affords you to make your life a gift.

ART OF MOTHERHOOD: EVE IN THE SISTINE CHAPEL

Now we have an opportunity to take inspiration from the Sistine Chapel, one of the most incredible works of art in the world. What do you think of when you hear "Sistine Chapel"? Do you picture Michelangelo lying on his back on scaffolding for twelve hours a day for four years, with paint dripping into his eyes? Do you picture 130 feet by 40 feet of bulging, sculpturesque figures? Do you think of the revolutionary moment in the history of art, leaving behind the typical composition of several people standing in a rural or classical setting acting out one scene, and now instead, hundreds of twisting, bulky people telling us the dramatic human story, all the way from Creation

The Creation of Eve (Sistine Chapel)

to the Last Judgment? The power, the drama, the glory of our tale jumps out at you and grabs you.

Maybe all you can really picture is the scene where God is about to touch Adam's finger. This truly amazing image is one of the most replicated works of art of all time. Adam, so dependent on God for his very life; God, so loving and personal, reaching out his tender hand. I feel the intimacy of God the Creator when I see this painting. It reminds me that God chooses to sustain me in every moment of my existence, and for that I want to give him praise.

The art historian Elizabeth Lev points out that, even though God's creation of Adam is the most noted panel in the Sistine Chapel, Eve is the center of this great narrative of humanity.[9] The ceiling has nine panels that run down the middle of it. The first three represent the creation of the world: *The Separation of Light from Darkness*; *The Creation of the Sun, Moon and Planets* (notice God the Father's bottom; he is "mooning" us — is this pious Michelangelo's sense of humor bursting out?); and *The Separation of Land from Sea*. Then the three in the center represent Adam and Eve: *The Creation of Adam, The Creation of Eve*, and *Original Sin and Banishment from the Garden of Eden*. The last three panels are dedicated to Noah: *The Sacrifice of Noah, The Flood*, and *The Drunkenness of Noah*. Note that the fifth one, the one in the center, is *The Creation of Eve*.

Is this significant? Is Michelangelo making a point here? When Michelangelo analyzes the human story, it revolves around a wife and mother. In *The Creation of Eve*, Eve is strong and graceful, a contrast to the lifeless Adam not yet animated. Furthermore, when you closely examine *The Creation of Adam*, while Adam lies lifeless, God's arm is wrapped around Eve. She is vibrant and alert, and caresses God's arm. God's intimacy with Eve is unmistakable. God already has her in mind, Michelangelo is telling us, this jewel of a creature ready to join Adam and form the first human community, a tiny reflection of the Divine Persons.

What is Michelangelo's overall message? What can we draw from the Sistine Chapel that will inform the artistic design of our own lives?

My personal experience of Eve in the Sistine Chapel is that the woman, wife, and mother are central in God's plan. God loves women, and God loves wives and mothers. Wives and mothers are not, as some misogynists would have it, second-class citizens, banished to the home and kitchen. Rather, they are key to God's creation and plan of salvation. They faithfully reflect the Godhead. The home and the kitchen are sacred places, where the human race is born and cultivated. Not despite being a mother, but precisely *as* a mother, a woman is powerful and important. She is the one from whom all of humanity is born and shaped. At the workplace, we have influence. At home as well, we are shaping the future. At our jobs, we are important, and under our own roofs, we are at least that important.

The Sistine Chapel is a reminder of the importance of family and motherhood in the sweeping drama of humankind. It is a reminder to me to keep my family at the center of my life, even when I am working outside the home. I give my out-of-the-home job the attention it is due and sometimes more than it is due. And I am reminded to focus on my family with my loving attention. I am reminded that, when so many other forces push and pull on my life, motherly care can never be overrated, and devoting myself to it is one of the most important ways I can spend my time.

THE PRAYER OF MOTHERHOOD: KNOW THYSELF

How do you know what God wants for you in this season of life, or what might he call you to down the road? Life is long, and it is a good idea to remain open to having several chapters in your life with distinct kinds of work and time in and out of the home.

As you discern God's calling for you, one tool for you is the wise axiom "Know thyself." This phrase was inscribed on the forecourt of the Temple of Apollo in Delphi in ancient Greece. It has been invoked by the ancient playwright Aeschylus, the philosophers Socrates and Plato, as well as many medieval and modern philosophers.

Additionally, the great mystic and Doctor of the Church, Catherine of Siena maintained that self-knowledge and knowledge of God are the two central tasks of the spiritual life. She recorded God speaking to her in her *Dialogue*, "Here is the way, if you would come to perfect knowledge and enjoyment of me, eternal Life: Never leave the knowledge of yourself. Then, put down as you are in the valley of humility, you will know me in yourself, and from this knowledge you will draw all that you need."[10] Catherine of Siena felt called by God to dwell in what she elsewhere called "the cell of self-knowledge." This is where she learned her limitations as well as her dignity, which also extends to the dignity of all human beings.

Because self-knowledge led her to an awareness of her limitations, she was propelled toward a greater dependence on God. Hence, self-knowledge and knowledge of God as the source of all good things are linked.

Self-knowledge led Catherine to a deeper awareness of the dignity of all human beings, including herself. This insight prompted her to greater passion in serving others. She also exercised rare courage in her efforts to bring about local civic peace and to persuade the pope, who had moved to France, to return to Rome. Self-knowledge helped Catherine to fulfill her capacities in building up the Church and serving those in need.

One way you can apply the wisdom of Catherine of Siena to your discernment of motherhood and work outside the home is to look at your motives and check them against the traditional list of virtues and vices. First, let's take up pursuing a career outside the home. What is your motivation for this work? How do you think God looks upon that motive? Are you seeking prudence in finances? Responsibility for student loans? Maturity? Independence? Are you called to use a particular skill, gift, or talent? On the other hand, do you see any vices in your motives?

Now look at this list of virtues and vices. The seven Christian virtues are: prudence, justice, temperance, fortitude, faith, hope and love. Do any of these speak to you as the bottom line regarding your motives as you design your life? The capital sins, however, are: pride, greed, wrath, lust, envy, gluttony, and sloth.

Be honest and reflect as to whether any of these sins is at the root of your motives regarding working outside the home.

Alternatively, let's take up staying at home with your children. What is your motive for that? How do you think God sees it? Again, look at the list of virtues and vices. Pray and use the tools from previous chapters, including *lectio divina* on your favorite Scripture passages, as well as the discernment of consolations and desolations in the manner of Saint Ignatius of Loyola. See what God is showing you about yourself. These are all good ways to reflect on your motives and make sure they are pleasing to God.

If there are people in your life who are *sure* that the only way to be a good Christian mother is to be a stay-at-home mother, or if there are people in your life who are *sure* that a successful woman works outside the home, I suggest that you set their messages aside as you begin the holy work of self-knowledge. Ask God to make you a saint. How will you be happy in the face of death? What will it take for you to flourish? What virtues does God most want to cultivate in you in this season of your life? What vices does he want to help you overcome? What kind of pressures might you be applying to yourself? Maybe you have inner voices far louder than the voices of people around you who are telling you how you ought to live and what raising a family ought to look like. Ask God how motherhood may or may not be part of your saint-becoming process, as well as what involvement in work outside the home, if any, God desires for you. May God bless you, and the Holy Spirit guide you, and may the intercession of Saint Catherine of Siena, as well as Mary the Mother of God and Saints Monica, Rita, Gianna, Zélie, and Elizabeth Ann Seton, be yours. May you be a part of a new era in which women creatively give to the Church and the world, not despite motherhood, but in and through it.

QUESTIONS FOR REFLECTION

1. Do you think that Plato's view of happiness and Aristotle's view of flourishing, though different, are compatible? Why or why not?
2. Are you flourishing, as Aristotle describes it? If so, what is a sign that this is true? If not, what is one thing that you could change that might facilitate your thriving?
3. What is your inclination or your decision about work in and outside the home? What ratio is best for you and those around you? What proportion of work and home do you think God is calling you to?
4. Which mother saint inspires you the most? Why?
5. In your opinion, does motherhood matter in the way Michelangelo's Sistine Chapel indicates? If mothers are central to human history and God's plan for humanity, how do you want to engage in that plan?
6. Describe where you are in your process of self-knowledge. What virtues are you achieving right now, by the grace of God? What vices is God prompting you to conquer?

— 5 —

BECOMING A
RADICAL CHRISTIAN

Now that you have considered your discernment in achieving personal fulfillment and happiness, have examined both your interior priorities as well as practical considerations, and have considered with utmost seriousness the issue of motherhood as it has a bearing on your doing something really great with your life, we will now turn to the spiritual life. Whether you choose to work full-time outside the home, full-time in the home, or anywhere in between, motherhood can deepen your faith and enhance your relationship with Christ. In fact, it can be the way you experience the radical Christian discipleship that marked the first generations of Christians in the early Church, who were so aflame with the

119

love of God and always looking ahead to the heavenly banquet.

For hundreds of years, many Christians, and especially Catholics, have believed that to be *really holy*, you had to be an overseas missionary, a mystic, a martyr, a monk, a nun, or a priest. You had to be celibate or brilliant or tortured or burned at the stake. But leaning in the other direction, some saints have proclaimed that holiness is for everyone. Saint Francis de Sales wrote on this topic in *Introduction to the Devout Life* in the seventeenth century, and there is a long legacy of preaching saints who went out to cities and villages on preaching missions to bring laypeople to holiness. The Second Vatican Council was a big moment in the Catholic Church when it made this message central: "The universal call to holiness" became an established teaching of the Church.

Pope Saint Paul VI speaks specifically of the important place of women in this universal call to holiness: "Within Christianity, more than in any other religion, and since its very beginning, women have had a special dignity, of which the New Testament shows us many important aspects. ... It is evident that women are meant to form part of the living and working structure of Christianity in so prominent a manner that perhaps not all their potentialities have been made clear."[1] The Church speaks of the universal call to holiness and exhorts the laity to cultivate an awareness of Christ as the fulfillment of all ordinary family and social life.[2] In fact, motherhood — as one aspect of family life — is sanctified by the fact that Christ entered into a family and thereby elevated to divine status his ties with his mother, and hers with him, as well as all familial relations. Hence, we are right if we see in the daily activities of family life, including all aspects of motherhood, an occasion to join ourselves to God.[3]

Many women fear the sacrifices that come with motherhood. Not only might you choose to make sacrifices in terms of your income or career, your lifestyle, your free time, and the chance to pursue your personal interests, but you will also likely experience physical hardships in pregnancy and childbirth and carrying a child around for the better part of two years. Yet these sacrifices are not setbacks; they are the very occasion for the fulfillment of your faith and union with God.

As you become more aware of motherhood, even in its sacrifices, as an opportunity for spiritual fulfillment, you will be helping the Church realize what Paul VI asked for: greater clarity regarding the prominence of women in the structure of Christianity. It is time for women, as well as laymen, clergy, and those called to the consecrated life to see the full spiritual meaning of motherhood.

We will begin by reflecting on how motherhood is fulfilled in Christ, especially through physical sacrifices. We will consider how motherhood has the possibility of being the vocation through which we find intimacy with Christ. In the Art of Motherhood, we will consider Grünewald's *Crucifixion*, which emphasizes the physical dimension of Christ's passion. Then we will discuss the Catholic practice of "offering up" challenges in a way that can be especially helpful to all Christian mothers.

INVITATION TO DIVINE LIFE

While all human beings have dignity and are called to greatness, the Christian has a better opportunity for greatness and a higher chance of success in accomplishing it than the non-Christian does. The Christian sees a horizon for greatness that is far wider and broader than most people are aware of. The Christian knows that

> the dignity of man rests above all on the fact that he is called to communion with God. This invitation to converse with God is addressed to man as soon as he comes into being. For if man exists, it is because God has created him through love, and through love continues to hold him into existence. He cannot live fully according to truth unless he freely acknowledges that love and entrusts himself to his creator.[4]

Christians have insight that most people don't: We have dignity precisely in being called to *communion with God*. God extends to each person the invitation to join the communion of the Blessed Trinity: "It pleased God in his goodness and wisdom to reveal himself and to make known the mystery of his will. His will was that men should have access to the Father, through Christ, the Word made flesh, in the Holy Spirit, and thus become sharers in the divine nature."[5] The invitation is God revealing himself. In Jesus Christ, God is saying, "Here I am. Here is the way to become friends with me."

When a person accepts the invitation and becomes a Christian, she makes the most magnificent choice possible for her. Not only does she get to enjoy fellowship with someone infinitely above her, but in the process, she is transformed into his likeness. She becomes like God because she is now a child of God, an adopted child in God's family: "God sent forth his Son … so that we might receive adoption as sons.

And because you are sons, God has sent the Spirit of his Son into our hearts, crying, 'Abba! Father!' So through God you are no longer a slave but a son, and if a son then an heir" (Gal 4:4–7). Adoptive mothers have an extraordinary way of living out a reflection of God and his love for humanity. Just as God adopts us and makes us his own, so, too, does an adoptive mother make a child who was once not hers now her very own. Now the child cries out, "Mama!" and is her heir. Adoptive mothers have a priceless and unique way of sharing in God's relationship of merciful love for us.

The Christian becomes a new creation: "If anyone is in Christ, he is a new creation; the old has passed away, behold, the new has come" (2 Cor 5:17). Divine life and fellowship with God: That is the life of greatness to which all are invited, but only a few accept.

For the believing Christian, nothing is more satisfying than finding one's particular way of living out the Christian life. Christians all have to live it out somehow. God has extended to us an invitation; our response is faith; that faith must be cultivated. We are blessed beyond words when we nourish our faith with the Word of God and when we increase our faith through works of charity (see Mk 9:24; Lk 17:5; 22:32; Gal 5:6; Rom 15:13). Faith is such a pleasure to cultivate because it is the beginning of eternal life. Saint Basil says: "When we contemplate the blessings of faith even now, as if gazing at a reflection in a mirror, it is as if we already possessed the wonderful things which our faith assures us we shall one day enjoy."[6] Faith on earth is a taste of heaven. We enter into an entirely new level of union with Christ when we find in our vocation a way to renounce the world and become more like Christ and obey his commands.

Sometimes these ways of renouncing the world and becoming more like Christ are concrete and even have physical or outward forms that involve some sort of physical suffering. The apostolic and post-apostolic fathers traveled and evangelized various regions around the world. Christian men and women suffered as witnesses to the Faith and sometimes as martyrs. Then, beginning in an earnest way in the third century, comfortable Christians — both men and women — left their surroundings and found more radical ways to follow Christ. Christians in Alexandria, for example, moved to the desert of Egypt and became hermits. Saint Anthony founded a monastery in the desert outside Alexandria, and his sister governed one for women. Some Christians chose an austere, hermetical life. Alexandra was one such woman; she shut herself up in a mausoleum for twelve years, reciting the psalms and praying, working with her hands, and receiving food from a woman friend through a window. She described herself many years later as "comforted whilst I await the end of my life in good hope."[7] Some Christians lived in little cells or apartments of their family's estates; others lived in cells with thatched roofs by a river. Some of them became trusted spiritual mentors and were sought out for advice by bishops and other members of the Church.[8]

One of the earliest monastic communities was founded by Saint Macrina the Younger and her brother Saint Basil the Great (whose brother Gregory we met in chapter 2). Their aristocratic parents had already been serving persecuted Christians. When their father died, Macrina assisted her mother in running the estate. Macrina dedicated herself to God and lived a life of asceticism. She influenced the whole family: She saw that her brothers Basil and Gregory were baptized; she educated them in theology (they called her "the Teacher"); and she encouraged them all the way to an ascetic lifestyle. They built a hospital and workshops in which the poor could make a living. Basil later wrote down their practices in what was called *The Short Rules* and then *The Long Rules*. Basil's emphasis on brotherly love, service, and humility inspired the Greeks, and later, the monasticism in the Byzantine Empire took him as their inspiration. Though Basil is often credited as the founder of Eastern monasticism, Macrina was seminal to the way of life of which he wrote.[9] Later, in the West, Saints Benedict and Scholastica, twins, left their classical studies in Rome; Benedict (480–547) lived as a hermit in Subiaco, while Scholastica chose a monastic life in Nursia. Benedict's Rule became the most famous in all of Europe, and thousands live by it today.[10]

MOTHERS EMPTIED OUT FOR OTHERS

Mothers, it seems to me, share in physical hardship by virtue of being mothers. The vocation itself demands of them sacrifices that are a reflection of Christ. In most cases, their physical suffering is a mark of being emptied out for others. Motherhood recalls the way Christ chose to be emptied out for us:

> Have this mind among yourselves, which was in Christ Jesus, who, though he was in the form of God, did not count equality with God a thing to be grasped, but emptied himself, taking the form of a servant, being born in the likeness of men. And being found in human form he humbled himself and became obedient unto death, even death on a cross.

> Therefore God has highly exalted him and bestowed
> on him the name which is above every name, that at
> the name of Jesus every knee should bow, in heaven
> and on earth and under the earth, and every tongue
> confess that Jesus Christ is Lord, to the glory of God
> the Father. (Philippians 2:5–11)

This passage is an early Christian hymn that Paul would have
learned from the earliest Christian communities; it is perhaps
the first summary of the essence of the Christian Faith.[11] The
heart of the mystery of Christ is his choosing to become lower
than himself, emptied out, to the point of death; and for this
he is eternally exalted.

First, taking our cue from biological mothers, if you examine mothers of any species, you will see that it is the sig-
nature of motherhood to be emptied for her young. A mare
will soon deliver her colt; the mare is heavy, swollen, and slow
in her gait. She has lost her agility. Her freedom to explore
and follow her natural curiosity has waned. When she lies
down in the pasture, she pants and rolls her eyes back as she
labors to deliver her offspring. While she is expecting and
then tending to her newborn colt, her life as she knew it is,
to a large extent, suspended, and her whole being — her in-
stincts, her hormones, her entire body, down to every cell, her
proto-intelligence, her intuition, and whatever kind of spiritual dimension she, as a horse, has — funnels its resources
into forming her young.

The human mother has the extraordinary opportunity
to see in this self-emptying a profound spiritual significance.
Motherhood, in most cases, is a matter of being emptied of
one's original life, physical abilities, and way of conducting

oneself in one's environment. As a biological mother grows in girth, she is diminished in her capacity to live life normally. She sets aside her life as it was, whether by instinct or by an act of the will or both, to do this monumental thing, which is the participation in the creation of new life. The vocation of a mother has this as its essence: being set aside or emptied for the sake of new life to emerge.

While the biological mother who procreates and gives birth does this in a physical way for the gestational life of the child, all mothers — biological, adoptive, foster, spiritual, step, and grand — are setting aside their lives and being emptied out for days, weeks, months, or years to come. Human mothers care for their young longer than any other species — in a traditional American home, eighteen years. Ask any traditional American empty-nester whether she has finished rearing her young, and she will smirk and say, "No way!" Rearing a child means protecting, feeding, keeping alive, educating, informing, modeling, teaching, disciplining, socializing, encouraging, advancing. It means helping a new person enter the larger community as a thriving, competent member who has something to contribute, and who is capable of the give-and-take relationship in the vast network of human society. This takes enormous time and energy. It is marked by generosity of spirit, a true pouring out of oneself in love for others, as reflected in Christ.

Women who struggle with infertility also have a share in Christ's "being emptied out" for others. A mother who carries this enormous burden usually could not know how many actual conceptions have or have not taken place in her body. She will not know until heaven. Has she seen specialists? Taken supplements, herbs, medicines, or shots? Endured countless tests, measuring hormone levels in her blood and urine? Has she had surgeries? Have her uterus or fallopian tubes been corrected or removed for any number of reasons? Has she been given the diagnosis of endometriosis, polycystic ovarian syndrome, luteinized unruptured follicle syndrome, premature menopause, or long-term unexplained infertility? Is she married to a man dealing with male factor infertility? Such experiences are not just medical or biological; they cut to the very marrow of a person's identity. Her physical journey of being emptied out for the child she longs for is intense and deep and finds its fulfillment on Calvary.

What of the mother who has had miscarriages? The blood tests, the ultrasounds, the pokes, pricks, and examinations. The recovery, the emotions, the hormonal fluctuations, the grieving. Women who miscarry have a share in physically being set aside and emptied for others. Like women who struggle with infertility, their bodies have been impacted in the initial stages of gestation or in the striving thereto, and their lives have been set aside for the incredible, passionate, deeply human anticipation, in heart, mind, and body, of new life. This is a significant participation in the vocation to motherhood, and shares poignantly ways in being emptied for the sake of another.

Once a mother has a child in her arms, that child is *in her arms*, which get tired — as do her back and neck. Sleepless nights leave her physically depleted. Her shoulders hunch over, and if she is lucky, she remembers to round them back out. Carrying a child in a carrier, a car seat, or a stroller; picking up a crying child, setting down and stabilizing a seated infant, laying down and tucking in a snoring baby are the sweet moments of motherhood that are almost always accompanied by physical stresses and strains. Motherhood never ceases to be physical: carrying, holding, swaying, reaching back, turning, twisting, grabbing, hugging, caressing, kissing. It may involve standing on the court or field sidelines for hours at a time, butterflies in her stomach, wondering whether her child will experience the exhilaration of victory or the humiliation of defeat. It may involve driving for hours at a time, every single day, so that her child can have the athletic, musical, artistic, educational, spiritual, and social experiences she desires for her child. She may sit for hours during long graduation ceremonies or dry tears from her eyes at her child's wedding. Almost everything about motherhood involves the body. More often than not, it is emptying oneself for someone else. Its true spiritual meaning is found in Christ's passion.

A mother has the opportunity to be intentional about giving herself to her child in so many ways. She has the chance to be like Christ, who "did not count equality with God a thing to be grasped," but "emptied himself." The human mother has the opportunity to reflect on this pattern and see in her motherhood the chance to reflect Christ. She can actively emulate him and willingly engage in setting aside, emptying, and pouring out her life in a plethora of ways, and in so doing, bring what is distinctively human to motherhood: her will, her intellect, her soul, her spirit, her heart. She can find in motherhood a way to lay down her life for others. "Greater love has no man than this, that a man lay down his life for his friends" (Jn 15:13). Motherhood can become a woman's way of engaging in this highest form of love.

The physical suffering of motherhood is specifically *for others.* Just as Saint Paul endured many physical pains as a result of his missionary apostolate, the physical challenges of a mother are the result of her maternal apostolate, her self-donation, her gift to another person. Her bodily experiences having to do with motherhood are generous. They are oriented to serve, build up, and nurture someone else. This is a Christological dimension of the physical aspect of motherhood that lends itself to seeing motherhood as an opportunity for Christian greatness.

Motherhood stands virtually alone in one similarity to Christ's crucifixion. Does a priest, cardinal, or pope shed blood for others by virtue of his vocation, by virtue of the sacrament of holy orders? No, his calling is sublime, but holy orders in itself does not involve the shedding of blood. Mothers of many kinds shed blood for others. Has a biological mother shed blood as she delivered her baby? Has a woman struggling with infertility bled — oh, too many times — in anticipation of new life? Not many vocations prompt such a thing. Is it not right to see in motherhood a tiny but singular reflection of Christ's shedding blood on the cross?

Furthermore, motherhood is unique in its conformity to the Eucharist. Does a woman nourish her children? Some mothers nourish their children with their own bodies, in the womb, and some through nursing. Is this not a faint image of Christ, who nourishes us and appropriates us to himself in the Eucharist? For adoptive, step, and spiritual mothers, if she cannot feed a child with her physical body, and for all mothers for the vast majority of their time in this role, she is the primary one who nourishes the child. Day in and day out, bottles, baby food, and then countless meals throughout the children's lives — does this not have a Eucharistic theme?

In so many ways, motherhood is patterned on Christ and is a vehicle for entering into a deeper relationship with him.

Paul writes, "I appeal to you therefore … to present your bodies as a living sacrifice, holy and acceptable to God, which is your spiritual worship" (Rom 12:1). This message takes on a particular meaning for mothers. In the varied ways that mothers suffer physically for their children, their love is manifest. This kind of love is holy. It is Christlike. Loving others even in one's flesh, being poured out as a libation for someone else (see Phil 2:17) is a supremely Christian act. Its spiritual dimension can be a primary way in which a woman finds and cultivates her relationship with God. Becoming aware of this dimension can transform her experience as a mother, and in turn, awareness of it can transform the Church by clarifying one way in which women contribute to the vitality of the Body of Christ — by living in the pattern of Christ's self-donation.

ART OF MOTHERHOOD: GRÜNEWALD'S *CRUCIFIXION*

The way that physical suffering can draw one to intimacy with Christ is a theme that artists have captured. A paradigmatic example is a depiction of Christ's Crucifixion made for the Isenheim altarpiece in the hospital chapel of St. Anthony's Monastery. Matthias Grünewald (c. 1480–1528) painted this crucifixion with stunning and gruesome details of Christ's physical passion.

The monastery hospital specialized in the treatment of an especially painful skin disease called Saint Anthony's Fire, or ergotism. It is a fungus that caused seizures, spasms, open sores, and often death. In an age without pain medication, Saint Anthony's Fire was especially dreaded due to the intense pain it caused. The monks of an order dedicated to Saint Anthony tended to those afflicted with this disease, helped them

Grünewald's *Crucifixion*, Unterlinden Museum, Colmar, France

endure their suffering, and gave them a dignified death.

Grünewald depicts Christ as having this same skin disease. Christ's skin is pocked with bleeding sores. His hands are contorted, and his fingers are curled upward in humiliating agony. His face shows physical distress — not spiritual serenity or humility, as is portrayed in so many other artworks. His body shows visceral anguish — not a regal or stately or handsome bearing, as is so often the case in paintings.

As patients were brought into the hospital, they were first admitted to the chapel in which this huge altarpiece hung. They would see Christ identifying with them in what they were enduring. They would see a Christ who, though equal with God, did not deem equality with God something to be grasped. Rather, Christ was willing to be made lower than himself. Not only that: He was willing to empty himself out and bear incredible pain, even to the point of death. Why?

In order to find us. To meet us where we are. To take on our suffering, our death, as his own, and to atone for our sins, so that we might live with God. He draws close to us through his body, taking on our sins to the point of death, and therefore, drawing us close to him in our bodies through our physical suffering.

This is a loving God. This is an empathetic God. This is a caring God, who, like a good shepherd, will go to any length to find a lost sheep (see Jn 10:11–18); who, like a good mother, will care for her child (Is 66:13); who, like a good father, will give his child what he wants and needs (Mt 7:9). This is a God who responds to us and reaches out to us in our afflictions, and who will show his love by taking on suffering to the point of death in his own body. Grünewald's altarpiece is a reminder that it is heroically loving to take on suffering in one's body for the sake of another person.

THE PRAYER OF MOTHERHOOD: OFFERING UP SUFFERING

Here is a tool to help you take on suffering for the sake of another person. I would honestly say, don't attempt motherhood without it! Many Catholics know about offering up suffering. Though it is less known to Protestants, this practice is conducive to all people who love Christ.

Offering up suffering has biblical roots: "I rejoice in my suffering for your sake, and in my flesh I complete what is lacking in Christ's afflictions for the sake of his body, that is, the Church" (Col 1:24). Inspired by this and like passages, many Catholics remember the suffering of Christ when they suffer physical pain, humiliation, mental anguish, rejection, or loss. And, in the midst of their pain, they ask that — by the grace of

God — their pain may be united to that of Christ on the Cross and offered to the Father.[12] In so doing, they become sharers in the redemptive suffering of Christ. [13] Their suffering is transformed, elevated, now participating in Christ's Redemption. It is not that Christ's Redemption is incomplete; but it is always open to all love expressed in human suffering. Our suffering thus mysteriously becomes efficacious for making reparation for sin and participating in the salvation of souls. In this way, our suffering becomes a beautiful ministry, a means of cooperating with God in his merciful love of humankind.

Examples of this redemptive notion of suffering are the two saints of Fátima, Francisco and Jacinta, who were visited by an angel three times before Our Lady appeared to them. The angel said, "Pray! Pray a great deal. Offer up prayers and sacrifices to the Most High." They replied, "How are we to make sacrifices?" He answered, "Make everything you do a sacrifice, and offer it as an act of reparation for the sins by which he is offended, and in supplication for the conversion of sinners."[14] These children, chosen as special instruments by God, were instructed to do as Paul writes in Scripture: to offer up sacrifices.

This tool is especially good for mothers. When my child drops a glass and it shatters all over the floor, I stop and think: What should I offer this up for? I sometimes include my children by letting them pick the intention. In my best moments, I let them see my hope and renewed spirit, so that they, too, can learn to resist grumbling, self-pity, and anger, and instead find a higher way, a Christian way, of handling life's disappointments.

Motherhood is the perfect environment for fostering the love of God through offering things up. Giving birth, toiling with adoption agencies and paperwork, scrubbing toilets, making dinner, teaching math facts, mopping floors, and washing dishes — these are the simple means through which the light of Christ can radiate into the world. Christ means to save the world, and mothers have a vocation that is designed to be a vessel through which his light can reach the darkness. Motherhood is perfect for bringing humanity to God. Offering up our daily lives, and the little (and big) crosses that we carry, is one way God's grace can touch the lost, the poor, and the brokenhearted. Yes, cooking dinner and folding laundry can be a means through which Christ saves the world.[15]

Offering up suffering is a practical way to spiritual greatness and ties in with the Little Way of Saint Thérèse, examined in chapter 3. Thérèse of Lisieux is a Doctor of the Church, and she expresses profound spiritual greatness in her prayer of self-oblation: "I offer myself as a victim of holocaust to your merciful love, asking you to consume me incessantly, … that I may become a martyr of your love, O my God!"[16] True Christian greatness, according to the Bible, means knowing how to embrace our crosses. Unlike the earliest Christians, who were persecuted and often martyred, contemporary Christians have forgotten, by and large, how to accept crosses and see in them the chance to identify with Jesus. Christ himself says in the Gospels, "If any man would come after me, let him deny himself and take up his cross daily and follow me" (Lk 9:23). The very heart of the Gospel is embracing one's cross. Jesus severely chastised Peter when Peter advocated Christ's avoiding the cross: "Get behind me, Satan!" Jesus cried (see Mt 16:23). Christ went on to explain that the cross is the very essence of his mission on earth. Embracing one's cross is the essential Christian virtue, without which one cannot grow in the fullness of the Christian life.

Motherhood is a lifestyle oriented toward embracing one's

cross. Motherhood may be the greatest vocation on earth for learning this skill, because a mother's love for her child impels her to enter into struggle and pain. Adoption, step-parenting, foster parenting, stepping in for a biological mother and taking up her role for a stretch of time — these paths involve joy because of one's love for the young one, but also offer the opportunity to embrace a cross. One is drawn in by the dignity and worth of the small person, but is also faced with challenges and self-mortifications.

If embracing crosses is the mark of spiritual maturity in the Christian Faith, then motherhood is a path to spiritual maturity. It is a vocation for sainthood. Let us blaze a trail of sanctity in our Church and in our world as we bring the unadulterated heart of the Faith to the world through our vocations as mothers.

QUESTIONS FOR REFLECTION

1. Do you think women have reached their full prominence in the Church?
2. Do you think of motherhood as being fulfilled in Christ?
3. Do you fear physical sufferings associated with motherhood? Are you open to seeing them as opportunities for growing closer to Christ?
4. Have you found your favorite ways of drawing closer to God and living out your faith? What are they? Are you open to motherhood as another one of them?
5. How does Grünewald's *Crucifixion* impact you?
6. Have you offered up suffering? What part does it play in your daily life of faith?

— 6 —

MOTHERS AS
WORLD CHANGERS

Not only can motherhood satisfy your inner longings and help you achieve personal happiness and new spiritual depth, and not only can you build up the Church through your engagement with the spiritual dimension of motherhood, but society is desperately in need of you as a mother. More specifically, it needs you to be a mother who is aware of the importance of her vocation, conscious of the positive influence her private actions at home can have on society.

We are now going to look at the notion of feminine genius as key to the enterprise of building a civilization of love and see how the Catholic Church implores mothers to "save the peace of the world." As you take up the role of motherhood in a new way, conscious of your contribution to society, you will be recovering what has been lost in the advancement of women, and helping to usher in a new era of justice and a full appreciation for femininity. In the Art of Motherhood, we will look at an icon that speaks to a mother's impact on the world. Finally, as a Prayer of Motherhood, we will apply the Novena of Divine Mercy to mothers.

MOTHERS CAN SAVE THE PEACE OF THE WORLD

Vatican II sends this message to women: "[Women], you are present when the mystery of life begins and console when life departs at death. ... You know how to render truth sweet, tender and accessible. Place the spirit of this Council in institutions, schools, homes and everyday life. Women of the universe, Christian or not, you to whom life is entrusted at this grave moment in history, save the peace of the world."[1] This passage refers to mothers who are present at the beginning of life — biological mothers conceiving and giving birth, as well as adoptive mothers taking children in their arms and promising to love and care for them as their own. And by extension, this passage can be applied to stepmothers, foster mothers, and spiritual mothers. A mother tends to have an openness and awe toward the life that unfolds and grows before her very eyes; she is predisposed to an intuition of the gift of the particular human life of her child.[2] She is set apart from those who default to measuring human worth only in terms of productivity, achievement, or material gain. In this way, mothers have a critical importance in offsetting the world's reductionistic calculus of human value. The Church recognizes the invaluable role mothers can play in reminding humanity of the great mystery that is human life.

Additionally, mothers have an essential role in rearing children in truth and virtue, fostering in the younger generation generosity, fairness, compassion, respect, integrity, and all the virtues upon which successful civilizations are based. Mothers are essential in the formation of society, their influence reaching institutions, schools, homes, and everyday life; in short, they are guardians of the heart, mind, and soul of human culture. Hence, the Catholic Church implores women to recognize their considerable collective influence and see that they have the power to "save the peace of the world," one child, one home, one vocation at a time.

CIVILIZATION OF LOVE

This message from the Second Vatican Council points to the way mothers can participate, specifically through their vocation as mothers, in accomplishing a main goal of the Catholic Church — as articulated by Pope Paul VI and all subsequent popes — which is to build "a civilization of love." This vision begins with Christ, who shows us that, just as God is love and we are made in his image, so we are made for love: to love and to be loved. It is the family — including mothers — who bear the largest weight of achieving this goal. Wives and husbands, mothers, fathers, and children have the essential task of cultivating, with the help of the Holy Spirit, relationships within the family that reveal the fundamental dignity of each human person. Having learned this manner of respecting one another's worth at home, human beings engage with the larger society and shape it.

John Paul II develops this theme when he says, "The future of humanity passes by way of the family."[3] He says, "The family is the first and fundamental school of social living: as a community of love, it finds in self-giving the law that guides it and makes it grow." As we saw in chapter 1, spousal love and the love that mothers and fathers have for their children reflect the interpersonal communion of the Holy Trinity. This love is rightly recognized, not as mere feeling or private sentiment, but as having profound theological and sociological impact. Society begins at home. Interpersonal love is the bedrock of the family, which, in turn, is the foundation of human society.

The people whom families send forth into society are the ones who will be our businesspeople, politicians, educators, professionals, and laborers in all sectors of the economy. Their way of relating to others, their values, their virtues, and their vices will become those of the larger society. The Catholic Church reminds us that it is in the family, where a mother's influence is deeply felt, that a way of relating that is loving, recognizing others as persons worthy of love, is learned. Only if the family takes up this task with intentionality will the building of the civilization of love truly begin.[4] It is in the home, where mothers play such a vital role, that virtues are cultivated. Society itself will not teach virtue. The business, political office, or job will not teach justice, mercy, honesty, fairness, or compassion. Businesses and various professional offices presuppose that the people they employ already have such virtues. Where else are they learned, but under the guidance of mothers, along with fathers and other caretakers? Mothers are the primary architects of society. They are urged by the Church to be deliberate in ensuring the moral dimension of the culture.[5]

FEMININE GENIUS

In building a civilization of love, women play a crucial role.

John Paul II coined the term "feminine genius" to express what women have that is crucial, in his view, to the salvation of peace in our world.

The feminine genius takes a cue from pregnancy: When a woman discovers she is expecting a child, in many cases she accepts and values the new life within her as a person. So often, an expecting mother intuitively grasps the value of human life in a heightened way. This experience gives rise to a certain habit of soul of seeing other people with the same dignity. Not all women become pregnant, and not all pregnant women accept the new life within them. Men can also have this awareness of the dignity of a new life, some men even better than some women. But John Paul II claims that the genius of women originates in a woman's maternal *capacity* — realized or not — to comprehend intuitively the dignity of the human person.

The genius of women also lies in the fact that women are more apt than men to be able to pay attention to the concrete human beings whom they encounter.[6] They are able to see them not only for what they can do for them — offering services and other advantages — but also as persons made to love and be loved. Mothers often have an especially heightened ability in this area, since they can imagine their own children taking any one of the roles they encounter.[7] They can see and appreciate the individual characteristics that make each person unique. Hence, women, and mothers in particular, have the ability to help society correct one of its most dangerous errors, an error that led right to the worst crimes, such as those of World War II: that of seeing people's worth only in terms of their measurable, economic value to society. Mothers have a vital role to play in helping society overcome its consumeristic, materialistic, nihilistic, and violent tendencies.

The feminine genius has a horizontal dimension, which is the inclination to defend and work for the dignity of the human person.[8] That is to say, many women are equipped to be leaders of the world in advocating for human dignity. This may take many forms, including political activism, education of various types, as well as prayerful intercession. The feminine genius also has a vertical dimension, which is to love God and see that Christ "fully discloses to man himself and unfolds his noble calling."[9] A woman's orientation to defend the dignity of human beings is well served if she is regularly "looking heavenward" to God, praying, partaking of the sacraments, and reading the Scriptures. There she finds Christ, the true basis of the conviction of the dignity of each human life. Without this vertical dimension, women exercising their feminine genius in serving the marginalized and the defenseless are likely to become exhausted in their efforts, whatever form they may take. This vertical dimension also prevents "objectifying" those whom one is trying to defend and keeps one's advocacy personal. When one seeks refreshment in Christ, one is better able to be nurtured and sustained in one's love for other human beings.[10] Thus it is the Christian woman who is especially endowed with a prophetic mission to infuse in culture an awareness of God that is crucial for preserving the humanitarian love necessary for peace.[11]

Catholic mothers, then, being aware of their Church's invitation to this noble calling of motherhood, and being primed by their experience as mothers to see the dignity of each human being in all his or her irreplaceable, concrete particularities, are paradigmatic as prophets for our times. Catholic and all Christian mothers can effectively move the needle for human dignity in our struggling world.

PRACTICAL WAYS TO MAKE A DIFFERENCE

Sitting at a desk in my high school classroom, I sensed the message imbued in the very air we breathed: *We are preparing you for greatness. We are grooming you to make a positive impact on the world. You are one of the chosen few, one of a slim percent of the next generation who will be able to do almost anything you set your mind to … if you take full advantage of what we offer.*

At the dinner table during those high school years, my stepfather would say to me: "Might you run for president someday? Maybe you should think of becoming a lawyer and then running for the Senate." He persisted with the same message to all of my sisters, and I deeply appreciate being perhaps among the first generation of young women who could have realistically dreamed of such a thing. My stepfather was a hero for helping our imaginations soar, and I relish in young women then and today knowing that it is a real possibility for any woman — maybe you.

Not taking away from this progress in the slightest, I now send messages to my daughters at my own dinner table: "Ladies, are you listening to God's calling for you? Listen to the promptings of your heart and for the stirring of his voice. Perhaps he will call you to some sort of leadership, such as through business, political life, even the presidency. Perhaps he will call you to a life of service, such as through ministry, education, business, or medicine. Perhaps he will call you to religious life — to be a bride of Christ. Perhaps he will call you to marriage, to motherhood, a powerful way to make a difference in the world. My best advice is to be love wherever you are: Become your best self, and then find the best way for you to give yourself away."

It was perhaps the biggest shock of my life to come to see motherhood as a powerful, culture-shaping vocation. As a young mother, I took a big risk to set aside my ambitions and focus on my children, a goal which to me felt unambitious. But as I followed the promptings of my heart and the stirrings of God's voice, I took that gamble and pondered where God was leading me. Instead of feeling underwhelmed and over-qualified for motherly work, I found myself captivated.

The captivating experience was that what I did in the privacy of my home could make a difference. Typically, when we think of power, the first thing that comes to mind is power over someone else. It is a vertical, top-down model of power. The president of the United States is one of the most powerful people in the world in this top-down sense, influencing legislation and, having the power to declare war, impacting people who are at the mercy of his or her decisions.

But as we saw at the beginning of this chapter, Paul VI and John Paul II refer to another kind of power, the power of influencing society from the ground up. The foundation makes all the difference for that which is built upon it; the roots have a determining influence on the whole organism. A mother's power, wielded through her vocation as a mother — holding a baby in her arms, strolling a baby down the street, pushing a child on a swing, picking up her child from school and helping her with homework, and so forth — is that she has the opportunity to imbue society with the values and priorities she deems best. She is an architect of society, a world changer, and she has the chance to make a significant impact.

I will appeal to Saint Thomas Aquinas to make this kind

of power clearer. In his *Summa Theologiae*, he describes what he calls an "exemplary cause."[12] A person creates something according to a design. The design can be external to him or her, such as a painter copying an external image he looks at. Or the design can be internal, an image in his mind or imagination. That image is the exemplary cause. It is the image that the creator aspires to attain in his creative work. Without this exemplar, there would be no product. Without a goal or design, the builder or artist does not even take up the hammer or chisel. The exemplary cause is powerful in the sense of being essential to the entire productive endeavor.

A mother has the power to discern and choose the exemplary cause for her family, and more broadly, for society. If we are to follow the imagery Aquinas has given us, a mother is a master builder. She has the opportunity to identify the goal for her family in asking herself, "What kind of people do we want to be?" She then raises her family according to these values.

The influence of mothers extends to the whole society. Human persons acquire virtue as their character is shaped throughout their upbringing. As we have seen, it is parents, caretakers, and mothers in a special way who determine the value system of a society. Having the power of the exemplary cause in identifying goals, mothers also have the power to execute these goals. In the following section, I will present three examples of ways I have seen mothering make a real difference in bringing virtues to life in my own family, which, in turn, will have their impact on society. I see my role as cultivating virtues not just for an immediate, practical gain within my home, but as a way of life that aims toward a contribution to the larger society — the fruit of which I may never see but I am assured is of lasting impact. I also offer these practical parenting reflections to reinforce for you that, even if you fear not being a good parent, a few good skills go a long way in achieving your desired effect of a thriving vocation as a mother.

Obedience

A book called *The Peaceful Home* sat on my coffee table for the first ten years of raising my family. It was an interior-design book filled with lovely pictures of simple, minimalistic home décor. It was not the photos (I'm not much of an interior decorator!), but rather the name of the book that gave me so much inspiration. I wanted a peaceful home, and that book kept me focused on the question "How can I render this home peaceful?"

My first answer to this question was that I wanted my children to respond obediently to my instructions. I wanted to get past crying, whining, and meltdowns whenever I said, "Please come here" or "Time to get ready for bed." The toddler hysterics ruined my peace and the peace of our home. I knew that my children would be happier, as would I, if we had a seamless, easy, "Mother gives instruction and child willingly obeys" kind of routine.

Like all parents, I did the usual offering of a treat or reward for good behavior: dessert if you finish your vegetables. Like all parents, I also gave the typical punishments for bad behavior: timeouts (one minute per year old) and the occasional spanking.

But one day, it came together: Offer a reward but warn of a punishment at the same time, a "double-pronged incentive." Offer a reward if the child obeys, but tell her what the punishment will be if she disobeys. If the reward is good enough and the punishment is bad enough, she will almost always do what you ask. For example: "Annie, if you put away all the books in the next five minutes you will get a star on the sticker chart. But if you do not, then you will get a timeout." As for incentives, we had a homemade chart with ten spaces per child. When the child did something good, she got a star. Ten stars in a row on this chart got her a sugar-free lollipop. From the age of three or four, this chart can be very helpful in incentivizing.

But when the incentive is not enough, and the child shows more resistance than usual, I do the double-pronged incentive. "If you do what I ask, you will get a star; if you do not, you will get a timeout." Over the years, the timeouts and rare spankings changed to age-appropriate punishments for the older children. Sometimes I have them drop to the floor and do push-ups. Sometimes they miss out on a treat, a dessert, or an outing. If a child is melting down over wanting to go to the park this very instant, I respond: "I cannot take you right now. But if you ask nicely and stop whining, I will take you tomorrow. If you continue whining, I promise that I will not take you tomorrow." My all-time favorite punishment, however, is to make the child do my most dreaded chore: cleaning up dog poop in the backyard. We have a big Golden Labrador. This dog leaves heaping, steamy messes in our yard, and I absolutely detest going out there with a plastic bag and cleaning it up. Once my children get to about age eight, making them clean up the mess is my go-to punishment. Five minutes of dog-poop cleanup is a very effective punishment for kids and teenagers alike.

The incentives have also adapted over time. We left behind the golden star stickers preschoolers love and replaced them with tally marks. I'd hang a piece of paper up with each child's name, and when they would do what I asked them to do, they would be rewarded with a tally mark. At ten marks, they would get a lollipop, a dessert, a movie, time on the computer, or something else they really liked.

After I had my fifth baby, our house became a little wild. I decided we needed to increase the incentives. One mother had told me, "Children crave time with their mother." This inspired me. I found a bag of poker chips collecting dust on a shelf and had each child get a sealable plastic bag and write her name on it. We kept the bags in a box in the kitchen. Whenever a child obeyed, she got a chip to place in her bag. Why poker chips? There is something helpful, I found, about a tangible reward, something bright and colorful, something a child can touch and feel. The children loved counting the big round chips in their bags. When a child earned ten chips, I took her on an outing, just the two of us. We usually went to the bakery, ordered a pastry and a drink, and sat and talked. I would ask that child about how she was doing, what was going on in her life, and let her open up and share with me what her inner world looks like. These were magical times. Ten years later, my children still recall to me how special those outings were to them.

The double-pronged incentive has been the only way Ron and I have managed to get our children to sit still and behave during Mass. "If you kneel through the whole consecration, we will make fruit smoothies when we get home. But if you wiggle off the kneeler or talk, I will take you outside and you will get a spanking." Or: "Please place your bottom on the seat and your hands folded in your lap. If you do this through Mass, you will get a Mento. But if you do not, you will have to sweep the porch." The rewards and punishments vary almost week to week, depending on what I can reasonably expect out of the particular child and what motivates him or her. Being smart about rewards as well as punishments takes some creativity, but also shows your children that you understand them and know how they operate. It is part of being tuned in to your children. The better tuned in to them you are, the better your ideas for rewards and punishments will be, and the more lighthearted and positive you can be about it, emphasizing the reward and how nice it will be for them to earn it.

The double-pronged incentive helps with the hardest of tasks in our home. It has helped with bringing little kids to public places, such as restaurants and adult functions. It has helped with homework and grades, cleaning up rooms, and teaching children to do dishes, laundry, and chores. It has helped with car travel and plane travel. A well-behaved family in public spaces blesses other people; it is a little way to make the world a better place. At age eighteen, my son exclaimed incredulously, "I remember traveling across the world and behaving on planes, trains, and taxis, all for one Mento!"

This way of raising my children is the single most significant way that I am impacting the society at large. As I said above, the inspiration came from the notion of having a peaceful home. This manner of parenting with a special view to obedience results in peace at home. Peace at home then leads to peace in the world at large.

Peace in the world comes when human beings know how to be together. It comes when everyone feels respected, acknowledged, and honored, when everyone feels important. It comes when there are no tyrants, no one person who always gets his or her way; instead, everyone cooperates, bending and yielding, so that everyone has a general knowledge of being respected. In a peaceful situation, human beings are free for community, free to love and be loved, and free to pursue their God-given needs, talents, and interests.

Peace in the world begins with peace at home. Tantrums and fits (of both toddlers and teens) stem either from the desire to dominate ("I want what I want right now!") or from the loathing of being dominated (e.g., "I am so sick of my sister always ignoring me, being condescending to me, or getting her way!"). When a parent teaches a toddler to be obedient, the underlying message the parent sends is that there are bigger and more important values than indulging oneself in the moment. The parent sends the message that each one of us has to learn to wait for what we want, to do sometimes what we don't always want to do, and to become aware of the people around us and how we impact them. Teaching obedience involves teaching cooperation and charity within a larger community. In a family with more than one child, it may mean teaching one child to be less tyrannical right now, while defending the dignity of the other one. It may mean teaching children to work together to keep a space tidy or to learn good habits. It almost always means seeking justice — that is, creating an environment where each person will be treated fairly.

Prioritizing obedience is, for me, ultimately, a way to love my children well. I have no desire to have obedient children so that, like trained poodles, they will sit and roll over on command. Instead, prioritizing obedience is for me a way of prioritizing their dignity. I want each of my children to know that I see and love them, and I want them to learn to love one another in action, not just in words. Parenting them this way has been a process that has brought us much closer and has enhanced their sense of dignity. My kids rarely get punished; much, much more often, they respond well to the incentives and earn them. So they get what they want, which is both the incentive (a lollipop or a new pair of shoes), as well as praise and the parental message, "You are behaving so well! Thank you, I appreciate that!" Requiring the best behavior from them turns into a way of loving them well.

More than that, my children are very close. My kids have learned to love being with one another. That is mainly because they know that each person is going to be treated fairly and with respect, and each person will get her wishes acknowledged and responded to in some form or fashion. Because they have a good sense of delayed gratification and of the greater good of the whole family, they are resilient and cooperative. They are team players par excellence. There are no winners or dominators. Everyone's interests are taken into account, and everyone gets his or her due.

The child who feels seen and heard, and who is required to bend and yield for the greater good, becomes a regulated, well-adjusted human being, capable of seeing the interests, needs, and dignity of the others. The well-adjusted child becomes a well-adjusted adult who continues to be able to see the needs of the people around him or her and bring peace throughout his or her lifetime. These are the kinds of people society needs, the kinds who will bring love, justice, and peace to those around them, making a positive impact on the communities, organizations, and societies in which they live.

Sharing

Siblings have the ongoing nightmare of living under the same roof with one another's toys, and children without siblings have to deal with the unexpected horror of a playmate coming over and picking up one of their toys. For most little children, someone even touching one of their toys transforms the most neglected toy in the bin, rather suddenly, into their "favorite."

As tiny tykes, my children Jacob and Mary yanked things out of each other's hands. The one to do the yanking would emerge triumphant. The other one would howl. They switched roles with savage ferocity. This went on and on. Of course, I told them to take turns. Of course, they resisted. And there I was, managing *every single minute* of their playtime. It was exhausting to the point of being almost debilitating. The idea of spending the next twenty years doing this was enough to drive me over the edge.

I took a deep breath and prayed. I offered up my frustration. I determined to find a way for my children to learn how to play nicely together without my involvement.

Enter a new rule. We have a Magic Question in our home: "When may I please have a turn?" If you ask the Magic Question, you will *definitely get a turn*. That's what's magical about it. The other child can take up to five minutes to finish playing with it. So, that child needs to tell you, "In one, two, three, four, or five minutes," or "Now." If they do not give you a turn, then I will take it away, and they lose the toy and get punished.

The Magic Question helps the child have confidence that, if he chooses the slower, longer route, he will get the toy. He is *sure* to get it, if he asks in a way that respects his sibling's need to finish her time with that toy. Additionally, the child who wants the toy is immediately punished if he does not ask nicely and give his sibling time to finish with the toy. Snatching a toy automatically results in *not getting it*. And the one playing with the toy *has to share it*. She gets a few minutes to wind down with it, and she is in control of designating how long, up to five minutes. But sharing is obligatory (except with a few prized things, such as a first Communion necklace, that all agree belong only to a certain child).

This rule took hundreds of times to enforce with these two children, not to mention the four who followed them. I could see their little faces as their brains processed it: *Asking the Magic Question is better than grabbing.* I daydreamed about overhearing them solve sharing conflicts on their own — a dream that came true in time. Older children eventually taught and enforced this rule with their little siblings, and it became a basic understanding for how our playroom operated.

Even at two years old, a child learning to share is learning to see the other person *as a person* who deserves his respect. As discussed in the previous section on obedience, the child is also, in this case, learning to be thoughtful rather than to overpower another person to get his or her way. The child learning that everyone deserves time with things he or she enjoys. The child learns that others, too, ought to have time with a nice thing, and no child is the center of the universe who can have and do whatever he or she wants all the time. The child thus learns a little humility, a little respect, a little justice, a little generosity, and becomes, in short, civilized and even well-mannered. These are virtues that we want our society to have. And where else but in the family do people learn these virtues? The art of raising human beings with virtue is critical business.

Speaking Kindly

Another challenge common to me and many parents is the tendency for children to whine, fuss, and yell. Every child does it, and every child has to learn self-control in this area. Learning to speak kindly when one is upset is an important skill for adults as well. It is the mark of a person who has the interest and ability to problem-solve and find genuine solutions to conflicts.

One of the hardest things about any family with multiple children is that older children feel more powerful than younger children, and younger children often feel slighted, brushed off, or disrespected by older children. Early on, I realized that I needed to correct this natural imbalance, because some of my younger children became rather hysterical: One whined ceaselessly; another stomped and fussed. I saw these younger children as fighting for justice. They were acting out to gain for themselves the dignity that was due to them and that they were constantly not getting. Motivated first by just wanting all the crying and storming to end, I asked myself how to help each child, no matter the age or birth order, to feel respected.

The first thing I did was make a house rule: *Use kind voices*. Whenever a child spoke rudely to a sibling, I would say, "Could you please rephrase that in a kind voice?" The boy who had shouted, "Mary, *give that to me!*" would rephrase it and say, "Mary, could you please give that to me?" Now, in a house full of teenagers, I still do it. A teen will fuss, "Give me back my hair straightener!" I chime in, "Kind voices, please." The teenager tries again: "Could you please give me back my hair straightener and, next time, ask me before you use it?" Infractions result in taking out the trash, a fine of a dollar, or, of course, the dreaded cleaning up of dog poop.

This rule applies to me as well. I try to speak kindly, but every once in a while, I blow a fuse and yell at my kids. At first, I felt rather entitled to do so. *After all, they can act so bad*, I would tell myself. But then I realized that we would never achieve a house without yelling and harshness if I were not included. So, when the oldest was nine, I announced a new policy to my children: If I yell, then I have to apologize to every person in the family and give each one of them a dollar. When I made this announcement, the kids' eyes got as wide as saucers. I explained, "We are going to have a peaceful home, and that means everyone speaks respectfully to everyone else, even when they are upset. That includes me." I recall well the first time the policy went into effect: I got very upset at how messy they had left their room, and even after I told them to clean up, it was a disaster. I yelled. Then I went into my room. I realized what I had done. I felt really bad. I went to my purse, got the money, and called the children together. "Kids, I am really sorry that I yelled. I should not have done that. Yelling is not how to get what you want." I handed each child a crisp one-dollar bill, even the two-year-old. They stood in amazement. Then I said, "Now, it is time to clean your room the right way." We went to their room, and I instructed and guided as they cleaned up every last LEGO and doll.

When you are upset, yelling or throwing a fit is a way of trying to get back the control you feel you have lost. It is my goal as a mother to teach all of us that communicating clearly and discussing conflicts with a spirit of mutual respect is the best way to get that control. It is not a kind of control over someone else. Rather, it is finding a solution that meets your needs in a way that preserves the good of the relationship or larger family or group. This is the kind of problem-solving that is critical for our society. Learning to get what you or your community needs, all the while maintaining peace and not dividing or rupturing relationships, is what makes for a thriving culture.

All three of these skills are interconnected: We are teaching a child to respect her parents by obeying them; we are teaching a child to respect her siblings by sharing with them;

we are teaching children and parents to communicate kindly to one another, no matter how upset they have become, and to stay committed to a healthy and reasonable solution. I consider these three virtues key to having a peaceful home, which will help my children be happy, thriving adults their whole lives. It takes some work, but that's okay. I expect mothering to be tiring and labor intensive. I expect to set aside my wishes from time to time to help and care for my children. But a chaotic home exhausts me in a different, more destructive way. A chaotic home grinds on me. A home with respectful, obedient children may take energy to run, but is life-giving, attractive, and enjoyable.

A peaceful home is the starting point for a peaceful world. As the Catholic Church has been so articulate about, a peaceful world begins with the family. A civilization of love begins at home under the care of parents and, often primarily, of mothers. Using parenting skills such as these is not just the practical, day-to-day routine of mothering; it has metaphysical and lasting significance. Mothering successfully can be part of a larger mission of bringing healing and transformation to our society, one child and one family at a time.

ART OF MOTHERHOOD: ICON OF A MOTHER'S ROYAL REIGN

The ancient icon of *Our Lady of the Sign* is a powerful image of Mary exercising a royal reign as queen over the world. Unlike icons in which Mary is looking down toward Jesus and holding him, such as in *Our Lady of Tenderness*, in this image she is looking at the viewer with her hands raised in prayerful supplication. In her lap is an aureole representing her womb, with Christ inside. He raises his arms, signaling

Our Lady of the Sign

that he is the King of heaven and earth, and Mary, as his mother, is queen.

For many centuries, Catholics have called Mary the Queen of Heaven and Earth. The original basis for this title goes back to an ancient Hebrew tradition of Davidic kingship, in which the mother of a king is considered a queen. In the Bible, King Solomon's relationship to his mother, accepting her as a powerful advocate, is clear:

> So Bathsheba went to King Solomon, to speak to him on behalf of Adonijah. And the king rose to meet her, and bowed down to her; then he sat on his throne, and had a seat brought for the king's mother; and she sat on his right. Then she said, 'I have one small request to make of you; do not refuse me.' And the king said to her, 'Make your request, my mother; for I will not refuse you.'" (1 Kings 2:19–20)

Bathsheba, the queen mother, has influence with her son as the second most powerful person in the kingdom. The king rises to meet her and bows down to her. She wears a crown and sits on a throne at his right side. The reason that the king's mother, and not his wife, has the role of queen is that, in those times, a king could have many wives. Solomon had several hundred — but he had only one mother. The mother of the Davidic king held great authority over the king's decisions. Scripture references the queen mother elsewhere, such as in the book of the prophet Jeremiah: "Say to the king and the queen mother: 'Take a lowly seat, for your beautiful crown has come down from your head. ... Lift up your eyes and see those who come from the north. Where is the flock that was given you, your beautiful flock?'"

(13:18, 20). The mother of the king is depicted as having a crown. The queen mother is an established part of the Jewish tradition as a powerful advocate.

As the Jews awaited a Messiah, a king who would liberate his people from captivity, Jewish women hoped to be his mother, not only for the good of bringing such a deliverer to the Jewish people, but also for the power it would bestow on her. Hence, the mother of the Messiah, Mary, has been called a queen ever since the earliest times:

> From the earliest ages of the Catholic Church a Christian people, whether in time of triumph or more especially in time of crisis, has addressed prayers of petition and hymns of praise and veneration to the *Queen of Heaven* and never has that hope wavered which they placed in the Mother of the Divine King, Jesus Christ … Mary, the Virgin Mother of God, reigns with a mother's solicitude over the entire world.[13]

This passage also references Mary as crowned in heaven and reigning "with a mother's solicitude" over the world. Just as Jesus' kingdom was not of this world, neither was Mary's. But many faithful have, for millennia, recognized her queenship as real nevertheless, and have seen her as a powerful advocate with her Son. That is why Catholics "pray" to Mary, which means simply to "speak to" or "ask": They ask for her as the Queen Mother to petition their case before Christ the King, seeing the power she has with him.

Our Lady of the Sign is based on the message of the prophet Isaiah: "Therefore the Lord himself will give you a sign. Behold, a virgin shall conceive and bear a son, and shall call his name Immanu-el" (meaning "God with us"; Is 7:14). This is the prophesy invoked by the Gospel of Matthew, describing Jesus as Emmanuel (see Mt 1:23). Hence the royal, messianic mission of Jesus implies Mary's status as queen mother. Luke, too, describes the angel Gabriel as appearing to a woman betrothed to a "man … of the house of David" (Lk 1:27). As we saw in chapter 1, the announcement is of a son whose reign will never end (Lk 1:31–33). Then, when Mary visits Elizabeth, Elizabeth greets her as the "mother of my Lord," a title used for the royal queen mother (Lk 1:43). Ancient and early-Church hearers of this gospel would have recognized royal undertones in this language.

In the icon *Our Lady of the Sign*, Mary is depicted as powerful over the world. Her raiment is fit for royalty, and her raised arms indicate her power of supplication before her Son. Additionally, the angels above her are a reference to the "Seat of Mercy" in the ancient Jewish temple, where God was present to the high priest once a year on the Day of Atonement. The Seat of Mercy was a lid on the ark of the covenant on which rested the cloud, the visible sign of the divine presence. Mary, the new seat of mercy, has Christ resting in her womb and then on her lap. Christ, the great High Priest and presence of God, is now present at all times.

This image, dating back to the eleventh century, with precursors reaching back to the fourth century, is a beautiful reminder not only of the importance of Mary in our faith and in the power of her intercession, but of the power of intercession of all Christian mothers. In the pattern of Mary, we, too, may pray for our world. With confidence, we petition Christ and ask for what we, endowed with feminine insight into what the world most needs, feel called to request.

We are world changers by virtue of our motherhood. Just as Mary was the one through whom the Prince of Peace entered the world, so, too, are we to usher peace into the world. As we discover the dignity of all human persons in the dignity of Christ, in whom we find our identity and calling, so, too, are mothers in a position to transform society by raising their children thoughtfully and virtuously and to be a part of bringing peace, justice, and love to others. Mothers can impart to their children and beyond the message that all people should be treated as persons made to love and be loved. Exercising our feminine genius, we can transform the world.

THE PRAYER OF MOTHERHOOD: DIVINE MERCY NOVENA

Mothers influence the world through their motherly care, instruction, and prayer. One especially powerful prayer is the Divine Mercy novena. You may be familiar with it: Saint Faustina recorded a series of visions of Jesus in which he revealed the Chaplet of Divine Mercy and promised that anything can be obtained with the prayer if it is compatible with his will. The novena is especially appropriate for a mother with a view to her larger social influence because, in it, one prays for all of humanity. The novena consists of praying the chaplet for nine consecutive days, with the following intentions:

- Day one: all mankind, especially sinners
- Day two: the souls of priests and religious
- Day three: all devout and faithful souls
- Day four: those who do not believe in God and those who do not yet know Jesus
- Day five: the souls who have separated them-

       selves from the Church
- Day six: the meek and humble souls and the souls of little children
- Day seven: the souls who especially venerate and glorify Christ's mercy
- Day eight: the souls detained in purgatory
- Day nine: souls who have become lukewarm

A person who prays this novena devotes each of the nine days to praying for one of these groups of people. As a mother, you can tap into your intercessory power for your family, but also well beyond the bounds of your home. As you cultivate motherly care not only for your children, but for the larger society as well, this novena can be one of your most successful tools in exerting influence with your children and with society.

The power of the chaplet upon which the novena is based is evident by its origin. In 1935, Saint Faustina received a vision of an angel sent by God to punish a certain city. She began to pray for mercy on them, but it was revealed to her that her prayers were powerless. Then she suddenly saw an image of the Holy Trinity, and these words appeared in her heart: "Eternal Father, I offer you the Body and Blood, Soul and Divinity of your dearly beloved Son, Our Lord Jesus Christ, in atonement for our sins and those of the whole world; for the sake of his sorrowful passion, have mercy on us."[14] As she continued praying this prayer given to her, the angel became weak and could not carry out the punishment. Later Saint Faustina received instruction to add the ending "and on the whole world." She began praying this prayer almost constantly; Christ described it to her as a "chaplet." The chaplet consists of the following prayers in this order, taking a total of about five minutes:

Our Father

Our Father, who art in heaven, hallowed be thy name; thy kingdom come; thy will be done on earth as it is in heaven. Give us this day our daily bread; and forgive us our trespasses as we forgive those who trespass against us; and lead us not into temptation, but deliver us from evil. Amen.

Hail Mary

Hail Mary, full of grace. The Lord is with thee. Blessed art thou amongst women, and blessed is the fruit of thy womb, Jesus. Holy Mary, Mother of God, pray for us sinners, now and at the hour of our death. Amen.

Apostles' Creed

I believe in God, the Father almighty, Creator of heaven and earth, and in Jesus Christ, his only Son, Our Lord, who was conceived by the Holy Spirit, born of the Virgin Mary, suffered under Pontius Pilate, was crucified, died, and was buried; he descended into hell; on the third day he rose again from the dead; he ascended into heaven, and is seated at the right hand of God the Father almighty; from there he will come to judge the living and the dead. I believe in the Holy Spirit, the holy Catholic Church, the communion of saints, the forgiveness of sins, the resurrection of the body, and life everlasting. Amen.

Eternal Father

Eternal Father, I offer you the Body and Blood, Soul and Divinity of your dearly beloved Son, Our Lord Jesus Christ, in atonement for our sins and those of the whole world.

For the Sake of His Sorrowful Passion (ten times)

For the sake of his sorrowful passion, have mercy on us and on the whole world.

Repeat the Eternal Father (once) and For the Sake of His Sorrowful Passion (ten times) for a total of five decades.

Holy God (three times)

Holy God, Holy Mighty One, Holy Immortal One, have mercy on us and on the whole world.

This chaplet can be said daily, especially at three o'clock, the hour of the death of Christ. Additionally, this novena is quintessentially to be prayed beginning on Good Friday and ending on the feast of Divine Mercy, the Sunday after Easter. But there is no reason why we cannot pray it regularly. It is an official prayer of the Catholic Church that is believed to be powerful in the eyes of God, revealed by Christ himself, as transforming and bringing mercy to the world. I cannot imagine a better resource for mothers as they resolve to "save the peace of the world" and build a civilization of love.

QUESTIONS FOR REFLECTION

1. Do you agree that God has entrusted humanity to mothers and that, as such, they have the power to build a civilization of love if they so choose?

2. What is the best parenting tool you have seen a parent use?

3. What is your reaction to the three mothering tools presented in this chapter?

4. What values or virtues would you hope to bring to the world through your motherhood?

5. How does *Our Lady of the Sign* impact you? Are you familiar with the notion of Mary as Queen Mother? What is your feeling about it?

6. Have you prayed the Divine Mercy novena before? If not, are you willing to try? If so, how might it impact your influence as a mother over the world?

CONCLUSION

A NEW FEMINISM

Recent decades have witnessed an incredible move-ment forward for women in society. John Paul II applauds many of the gains for women achieved by the feminist movement:

> The role and dignity of woman have been espe-cially championed in this century by the femi-nist movement. It has sought to react, sometimes in forceful ways, against everything in the past and present that has hindered the full apprecia-tion and development of the feminine personal-ity as well as woman's participation in the many expressions of social and political life. These demands were in large part legitimate and con-tributed to building up a more balanced view of

> the feminine question in the contemporary world.
> The Church … has paid special attention to these
> demands, encouraged by the fact that the figure of
> Mary, if seen in the light of her Gospel life, is a valid
> response to woman's desire for emancipation. Mary is
> the only human person who eminently fulfills God's
> plan of love for humanity.[1]

This is an era in which women's presence in all areas of our
economy and culture is benefiting our society. Some of the
benefit is in the intelligence, skill, and talent of women making their mark. Additionally, having women in the public
sector forces systems to redesign themselves, so that they are
not exclusively oriented toward efficiency and productivity,
but are more accommodating of personal and familial health
and flourishing.[2] This is better for the women and men in our
workforce, and for the health of society as a whole. The ad-
vances of feminism also benefit women in that they finally
have the chance to cultivate all the aspects of their intellect,
talent, and creativity.

The next level of advancement for women, however, is
for this improvement to continue — since justice is not yet
achieved in this area and progress for women's presence in
industry is still in process — all the while bringing motherhood into the foreground. The culture needs to take a quantum leap in how it sees motherhood, not as a setback, but as
a movement forward; not as a threat, but as a benefit. This
quantum leap in the culture will happen if women take the
leap themselves. When women become aware of the value of
their motherhood for themselves, their children, their larger
families, and the society, and when their language and choices

show this awareness, society will adapt. A change in one person's attitude is the beginning of a cultural revolution. This revolution, in two words, is the awareness that *motherhood matters.*

THE WORLD NEEDS A MOTHER'S TOUCH

Once a year, I go on a week-long prayer retreat. When I come home, my husband and children always say, "We are *so glad* you are back. We *need* you." A mother's presence is irreplaceable. No matter how hard my husband has tried, no matter how noble his efforts, a child with skinned knees needs his mother's reassurance, teenagers need a mother's intuition, meals need a mother's oversight, and the home needs a mother's touch.

The world is like that; it needs mothers. It needs mothers who know that their work *as mothers* — whether or not they work outside the home as well — is irreplaceable. It needs mothers who are proud to be mothers and who mother with assurance that what they do for one child, they do for the world. Every moment spent bonding with a child, loving and appreciating that child, is a moment that brings love, health, and the presence of God into society. Every moment spent correcting a child and teaching him patience, generosity, and compassion is a moment that forms well-adjusted people who will soon enter into the larger structure of society.

Imagine a society that runs an experiment: No one can have sex in this society. Therefore, no one reproduces. The result is obvious: The society would quickly disappear. It is a stupid experiment. Well, a society that sets aside motherhood, discouraging motherhood and making a woman feel second-rate or inferior because she is a mother, is just as bad an idea. A healthy society needs good mothers, mothers who give their best to motherhood, mothers who love being mothers. The world needs mothers who know their importance and value to the larger society.

NEW FEMINISM

Many young women today publicly distance themselves from the label "feminist." They associate feminism with male-bashing and man-hating; with a loss of femininity; with an ideology that says that women have to become like men in order to succeed; with being militant, harsh, and, on the whole, unfriendly.

But if you ask any of those women, most of them would say that they are against gender discrimination, sexual harassment, and less pay to an employee based solely on her gender. Most of them would say that a woman's place is not only in the home, and that women make outstanding professionals, CEOs, doctors, lawyers, politicians, school principals, and so forth. Most of them take it hard when a woman has to work twice as hard as her male counterpart to earn the respect of her peers, and they rejoice when a woman is at the top of her field, whatever the field.

These women are great candidates for the "new feminism," a Christian form of feminism that appreciates and respects femininity. John Paul II initiated the use of this term (which was used differently in the 1920s) when he said:

> It depends on [women] to promote a "new feminism" which rejects the temptation of imitating models of "male domination," in order to acknowledge and affirm the true genius of women in every aspect of

the life of society and overcome all discrimination, violence, and exploitation. … You are called to bear witness to the meaning of genuine love, of that gift of self and of that acceptance of others which are present in a special way in the relationship of husband and wife, but which ought also to be at the heart of every other interpersonal relationship.[3]

Since his promotion of a "new feminism" here and in other writings, Christian women who are pro-life, pro-woman, and minded toward justice for women have developed this platform.

Proponents of the new feminism believe the following:

- Women make a valuable contribution in the workplace.
- Not being identical with men, women have a unique contribution to make to society.
- That contribution is the "feminine genius," that women tend to be respectful of people, not for their usefulness, but as people inherently deserving of respect.
- Women tend to bring an element of humanness and personal care to otherwise profit-oriented environments.
- Women and men should both be appreciated for their various positive contributions to society.
- Women and men are not identical, nor is one superior to the other.
- Family is crucial to society, and healthy families result in a healthy world.

- Motherhood, fatherhood, and marriage are all valuable to society and should be protected and respected.
- Mothers, including working mothers and stay-at-home mothers, are essential to our society and should be appreciated.
- To be pro-life is to be pro-woman.

The new feminism appreciates and retains many of the benefits that the feminist movement has procured for women and thus for society. It distinguishes itself, however, in its heightened appreciation of motherhood, in its Christian values of kindness, respect, and compassion, and in being pro-life. It is, in my view, compatible with and necessary for the building of a civilization of love.

SEISMIC SHIFT FOR WOMEN: MUTUAL SUPPORT

When women and men accept the tenets of this new feminism, a seismic shift happens: Women support one another. Working mothers support stay-at-home mothers; stay-at-home mothers support working mothers. Men, too, support all the choices women make in terms of creatively designing masterpieces with their lives. When the platform is "Women should stay at home" or, alternatively, "Women should advance their place in the workforce," women divide against each other, and men consequently divide as well. But when the platform is elevated to seeing each woman as being made in the image of God, having a spark of divine creativity, and giving her gift as God calls her to, division transforms into unity. Not all women use their creativity well, just as not all men use their talents well. Not all people are making a positive contribution. The new feminism does not gloss over sin and vice; it does, however, make room for all women to excel in creatively designing their lives. And it supports other women in doing so, applying the Golden Rule: Treat others as you want them to treat you. Give them the same freedom to design their lives, with regard to family life, motherhood, and work outside the home, as you hope they will extend to you.

This is a worldview that brings peace to families because it is wide enough to pass on to future generations. Grandmothers, mothers, daughters, daughters-in-law, adoptive mothers, foster mothers, and stepmothers all have a legitimate place in the new feminism. They don't have to fight against each other, with younger women separating themselves from older generations to distinguish themselves as working outside the home; older women looking with disdain on mothers who work outside the home; biological mothers being seen as superior to or more legitimate than stepmothers, adoptive mothers, or foster mothers, and so on. When the platform is *appreciating the feminine genius, however it is creatively applied*, tensions dissolve.

It is also a platform that is broad enough to include women and mothers of all races. Though some accused the feminism of the 1960s and '70s of not being sensitive to the prejudices against nonwhite women, the new feminism includes women of all races, ethnicities, cultures, and ages. Being based on the dignity of the human person, it is open to all human beings and is supportive of their advance in the world through motherhood, through working in the public workplace, and through the genuine exercise of the feminine genius.

YOU ARE A PROMISE

You are a woman who wants to do something great with your life. I want that too — I want you to flourish. The world

174 A New Feminism

needs you to be great. It needs you to become the fullness of who you are meant to be, to actualize your potential.

When I was a little girl, I had a Christian record (literally a vinyl record) by the Bill Gaither Trio. They sang a song called "I Am a Promise":

> I am a promise.
> I am a possibility.
> I am a promise—with a capital "P."
> I am a great big bundle of potentiality!
> I am learning to hear God's voice,
> And I am trying to make the right choice.
> I can do anything — anything God wants me to do.[4]

This is the message, summed up in a short children's song. You, precious child of God, are a great big bundle of potentiality. Set your sights firmly on a civilization that prioritizes the dignity of the human person and the dignity of women. Hold firmly to these axiomatic principles, and everything else will fall into place. Like Saints Gianna and Zélie and other women saints, your modern life can be bold and beautiful. It can be productive and motherly. You can blossom as a professional and as a mother. Just ask for lots of help and surround yourself with people who appreciate your feminine genius. Choose as your friends and companions people who support your vocation to family. Discern God's calling for you each step of the way.

My prayer for you is found in Scripture: "May [God] grant you your heart's desire, and fulfill all your plans! / May we shout for joy over your victory. / ... Now I know the LORD will help his anointed" (Ps 20:4–6). Keep this passage close to your heart, as I am keeping it close to mine for you. Let us look forward to the great banquet in heaven, where we can greet each other. Let us then share with one another the amazing works of love and creativity that God accomplished in our lives, the unmistakable ways that he used us to build the kingdom of God and the civilization of love.

Notes

Introduction

1. Gloria Steinem, *The Truth Will Set You Free, but First It Will Piss You Off!* (New York: Random House, 2019), 15, Kindle ed.

Chapter 1

1. John Paul II, *Letter to Families* (Manchester, NH: Sophia Institute for Teachers, 2015), chap. 1, par. 6.

2. Homily of His Holiness John Paul II (January 28, 1979), Palafox Major Seminary, Puebla de Los Angeles, Mexico, Congregation for the Clergy, http://www.clerus.org/bibliaclerusonline/en/f4c.htm.

3. John Paul II, *On the Dignity and Vocation of Women: Mulieris Dignitatem* (Boston: St. Paul Books and Media, 1988), chap. 3, par. 6. Also see John Paul II, *Letter to Families*, chap. 1, par. 6.

4. John Paul II, *Theotokos: Woman, Mother, Disciple* (Boston: Pauline Books and Media, 2000).

5. John Paul II, *Letter to Families*, chap. 1, par. 6.

6. Ibid. Also see Karol Wojtyla, *Love and Responsibility* (San Francisco: Ignatius Press, 1993), 33.

7. John Paul II, *Letter to Families*, chap. 1, par. 7.

8. John Paul II, *On the Dignity and Vocation of Women*, chap. 6, par. 19.

9. See also Second Vatican Council, *Lumen Gentium*, accessed January 6, 2021, Vatican.va, par. 54; John Paul II, *Theotokos*, 55.

10. John Paul II, *On the Dignity and Vocation of Women*, chap. 2, par. 3.

11. Ibid., quoting Second Vatican Council *Nostra Aetate*, accessed January 6, 2021, Vatican.va, par. 1.

12. *On the Dignity and Vocation of Women*, chap. 2, par. 3.

13. Ibid.

14. Ibid., quoting *Nostra Aetate*, par. 2.

15. *On the Dignity and Vocation of Women*, chap. 2, par. 4.

16. Ibid.

17. John Paul II, *Letter to Artists*, accessed January 6, 2021, Vatican.va, par. 1.

18. Jean Leymarie, Herbert Read, and William S. Lieberman, William S., *Henri Matisse* (Berkeley: University of California Press, 1966), 9.

19. In fact, I have co-written a Mother's Rosary Guide to help you deepen your faith and find greater encouragement in your life as a mother through the Rosary. See *A Mother's Rosary* at https://mightyishercall.com/products/#Products/Ebooks.

CHAPTER 2

1. John Paul II, *Letter to Artists*, par. 1.

2. Henri de Lubac, SJ, *The Drama of Atheist Humanism* (San Francisco: Ignatius Press, 1995), 22–23.

3. Ibid., 23.

4. *The Autobiography of Saint Margaret Mary Alacoque* (Rockford, IL: TAN Books, 1986), par. 6.

5. Ibid., par. 16.

6. Ibid. See also pars. 22, 25, 28.

7. Ibid., par. 16.

8. Ibid., par. 25.

9. Ibid., par. 35.

10. Ibid., par. 48.

11. Ibid., par. 52.

12. Ibid.

13. Gregory of Nyssa, *Sermons on the Beatitudes*, Sermon 3, paraphrased by Michael Glerup (Downers Grove, IL: InterVarsity

Press, 2012), 52. See also Gregory of Nyssa, *From Glory to Glory: Texts from Gregory of Nyssa's Writings*, trans. Herbert Musurillo, SJ (Crestwood, NY: St. Vladimir's Seminary Press, 1995), 88.

14. Gregory of Nyssa, *The Great Catechetical Oration*, Nicene and Post-Nicene Fathers, Second Series, vol. 5, ed. Philip Schaff and Henry Wace (Old Chelsea Station, New York: Cosimo Classics, 2007), par. 5.

15. Ibid.

16. Saint Thomas Aquinas, *Summa Theologiae*, trans. Fathers of the English Dominican Province (Westminster, MD: Christian Classics, 1981), I, q.19, a.1.

17. See Raissa Maritain, *We Have Been Friends Together: Memoirs*, trans. Julie Kernan (New York: Longmans, Green, 1942).

18. *The Autobiography of Saint Margaret Mary Alacoque*, par. 23.

19. David Fleming, SJ, *The Spiritual Exercises of Saint Ignatius: A Literal Translation and a Contemporary Reading* (Saint Louis: Institute of Jesuit Sources, 1987). The following section draws from Ignatius's primary text as well as from Father Fleming's commentary.

CHAPTER 3

1. For a delightful exploration of these and other kinds of love, see C. S. Lewis, *The Four Loves* (New York: Harcourt Brace Jovanovich, 1960).

2. Plato, *Phaedo*, trans. G. M. A. Grube (Indianapolis: Hackett, 1977).

3. Tertullian, *The Passion of the Holy Martyrs Perpetua and Felicity*, trans. R. E. Wallis (Gaeta, Italy: Passerino Editore, 2019), Kindle ed.

4. Viktor Frankl, *Man's Search for Meaning* (Boston: Beacon Press, 1959), 48-49, emphasis mine.

5. Avery Dulles, "John Paul II and the Mystery of the Human Person," *America*, February 2, 2004, accessed January 6, 2021,

https://www.americamagazine.org/issue/469/article/john-paul-ii
-and-mystery-human-person.

6. John Paul II, *Love and Responsibility* (San Francisco: Ignatius Press, 1993), 82.

7. Second Vatican Council, *Gaudium et Spes*, accessed January 6, 2021, Vatican.va, par. 24; John Paul II, *Letter to Families*, chap. 1, par. 11.

8. *On the Dignity and Vocation of Women* , chap. 3, par. 7.

9. Ibid., chap. 6, par. 18.

10. Ibid.

11. Ibid., emphasis mine.

12. Ibid.

13. Pope Benedict XVI, *Deus Caritas Est*, accessed January 6, 2021, Vatican.va, par. 6.

14. Ibid., par. 9.

15. Ibid., par. 3.

16. Ibid., par. 7.

17. Ibid., par. 11.

18. *Saint Thérèse of Lisieux: An Autobiography* (New York: P. J. Kenedy and Sons, 1926), 151.

19. Ibid., 152.

20. Ibid., 154.

21. Ibid., 168.

22. Ibid., 187.

23. Ibid., 164.

24. Ibid., 166.

Chapter 4

1. Aristotle, *Nichomachean Ethics*, in *The Complete Works of Aristotle*, revised Oxford translation, ed. Jonathan Barnes, vol. 2 (Princeton: Princeton University Press, 1984), 1100b18–20; 1101a6.

2. Ibid., I.9.1099b10; II.1.1103a15–17, 32.

3. Aristotle, *De Anima*, trans. Mark Shiffman (Newburyport, MA: Focus Publishing/R. Pullins, 2011), II.4.415b1–8.

4. See Peggy Andrews, "How Mothers with Professional Careers Experience the State of Flourishing," in *Woman as Prophet in the Home and in the World*, ed. Mary Hayden Lemmons (Lanham, MD: Lexington Books, 2016).

5. Pietro Molla and Elio Guerriero, *Saint Gianna Molla* (San Francisco: Ignatius Press, 2004), 54–55.

6. Many thanks to Christine Baglow, member of the Saint Gianna Beretta Molla Society, for her advice on this section.

7. All statistics in this section, unless otherwise noted, are taken from the U.S. Department of Labor, 2016.

8. Megan Brenan, "Record-High 56% of U.S. Women Prefer Working to Homemaking," Gallup, October 24, 2019, accessed January 6, 2021, https://news.gallup.com/poll/267737/record-high-women-prefer-working-homemaking.aspx.

9. Elizabeth Lev, "The Unheard Story behind the Sistine Chapel," TED Talk, February 12, 2016, accessed January 6, 2021, https://youtu.be/lQflBowgVB4.

10. Catherine of Siena, *The Dialogue*, trans. Suzanne Noffke, OP, Classics of Western Spirituality (New York: Paulist Press, 1980), 4, 29.

Chapter 5

1. Paul VI, Address to Participants at the National Meeting of the Centro Italiano Femminile (December 6, 1976), accessed January 6, 2021, Vatican.va; *Insegnamenti di Paolo VI* XIV (1976): 1017.

2. John Paul II, *The Lay Members of Christ's Faithful People: Christifideles Laici* (Boston: Pauline Books and Media, 1988), par. 14.

3. Ibid., par. 17.

4. Second Vatican Council, *Gaudium et Spes*, par. 1.

5. Second Vatican Council, *Dei Verbum*, accessed January 6, 2021, Vatican.va, par. 2; cf. Eph 1:9; 2:18; 2 Pt 1:4.

6. Saint Basil, *De Spiritu Sancto, The Treatise De Spiritu Sancto and the Nine Homilies of the Hexaemeron*, Nicene and Post-Nicene Fathers, Second Series, vol. 8, ed. Philip Schaff (Buffalo: Christian Literature Company, 1886), 15, 36.

7. Laura Swan, *The Forgotten Desert Mothers: Sayings, Lives, and Stories of Early Christian Women* (New York: Paulist Press, 2001), 72.

8. Ibid., 79, 81, 100.

9. Ibid., 128.

10. David Knowles, *Christian Monasticism*, World University Library (New York: McGraw-Hill, 1969).

11. Richard Bauckham, *Jesus and the God of Israel: God Crucified and Other Studies on the New Testament's Christology of Divine Identity* (Grand Rapids, Michigan: William B. Eerdmans Publishing Company, 2008), 41

12. Paul Mihalik, OCDS, M.Ed., *Offering of Suffering* (Goleta, CA: Queenship Publishing, 2000), 4.

13. Ibid., 22, quoting John Paul II's apostolic letter *Salvifici Doloris*.

14. Mihalik, *Offering of Suffering*, 11.

15. Second Vatican Council, *Lumen Gentium*, par. 3.

16. Mihalik, *Offering of Suffering*, 97.

CHAPTER 6

1. Second Vatican Council, The Council's Message to Women (December 8, 1965), *Acta Apostolicae Sedis* 58 (1966), 13–14, trans. R. Mary Hayden Lemmons.

2. John Paul II, *The Genius of Women* (Washington, DC: USCB Publishing, 1997), 25.

3. John Paul II, *The Role of the Christian Family in the Modern World: Familiaris Consortio* (Boston: Pauline Books and Media, 1981), 64.

4. Ibid., 13.

5. John Paul II, *The Lay Members of Christ's Faithful People*, 51.

6. John Paul II, *On the Dignity and Vocation of Women*, chap. X, par. 18.

7. Susan C. Selner-Wright, "St. John Paul II and the Genius of Women," in *Woman as Prophet in the Home and with World*, ed. R. Mary Hayden Lemmons (Lanham, MD: Lexington Books, 2016).

8. Ibid., 34.

9. Second Vatican Council, *Gaudium et Spes*, par. 34.

10. Lemmons, *Woman as Prophet in the Home*, 34.

11. Ibid.

12. *Summa Theologiae*, I, q.44, a.3.

13. Pius XII, *Ad Caeli Reginam*, accessed January 6, 2021, Vatican.va, par. 1, emphasis mine.

14. *Diary of Saint Faustina Kowalska: Divine Mercy in My Soul* (Stockbridge MA: Marian Press, 2005), par. 475.

CONCLUSION

1. John Paul II, *Theotokos*, 42.

2. John Paul II, *Letter to Women* (Boston: St. Paul Books and Media, 1995), 4.

3. John Paul II, *Evangelium Vitae*, accessed January 6, 2021, Vatican.va, par. 99.

4. William J. Gaither and Gloria Gaither, "I Am a Promise," copyright © 1975 Hanna Street Music (BMI) (adm. at CapitolCMG-Publishing.com). All rights reserved. Used by permission.

ACKNOWLEDGMENTS

That this book exists is a wonder. Without the un-flagging support and generous prayers of many people, it simply would not be. Many weekends, my husband whisked all our kids out of town to visit his family. Sometimes they quipped, "We don't believe you are married to Kathryn anymore!" I was at home, plugging away on this book while they all rode horses and had shrimp boils. Even at home, how many mornings did my husband say, "How can I help you get some writing time today?" How many times did he run a carpool, take kids to jiujitsu or make pancakes on a Saturday in order to give me a chance to write? Thank you, Ron.

My children have touched me so deeply in their support and enthusiasm for this book. My eldest, Jacob, has a new refrain: "I cannot believe that after ten years of seeing your binders on the shelves labeled 'Motherhood' and after all these years of you working so hard on it, it is finally in print! I am so happy for you!" My daughters as well marvel and celebrate. I have been motivated by them, hoping to express in writing why I have given my life to them and why I believe this vocation is worthy of serious discernment. They seem to take it as a gift directly for them. Thank you, kids.

My mom has been single-visioned and pure of heart in her support of me writing this book. She has been altruistic, generous, and perhaps my biggest fan. Thank you, Mom.

My dad, siblings, and extended family have been so supportive. My sister, Kimberly June Miller, read this manuscript in its entirety and gave invaluable insight and feedback. Thank you, Kim, and all my family.

My friends in and around Covington, Louisiana, told me fifteen years ago, "Kathryn, you have to write a book!" They were this book's original inspiration. Christine Baglow, Ashleigh Gervais, Jennifer Hayes, Patricia Phillippi, Mary Beth Russell, Lauren Sanborn, Anne Simpson, and Char Young: Thank you for your friendship, love, and prayers.

My friends in Irving, Texas, have been nothing short of amazing. Anna Dunikoski met with me every few weeks and asked about my progress — for years! She never ran out of hope or encouragement. Thank you, Anna.

Rebecca Sanford and Susanna VanVickle prayed with me many times, earnestly petitioning the Lord for abundant grace for this project. Their confident assurance that this book would come to fruition has been invaluable. Susanna gave a gift such that, in all earnestness, this book would not exist if it were not for her. She took the helm of the nonprofit I am a part of, Mighty Is Her Call, Inc., a ministry for Catholic mothers. If she had not given her heart and soul to that ministry for the better part of a year, I would not have had the chance to write the final draft of this book. Jolly Hormillosa, too, has given her gifts to this ministry and to me, and to her I will forever be indebted. Thank you, Rebecca, Susanna, and Jolly.

I have been so blessed by Heidi Saxon, Mary Beth Baker, and Rebecca Martin. I cannot thank OSV enough for being a wonderful press to work with. I am grateful to Sr. Mary Angelica Neenan, Lynn Schofield and James DeMasi for reading sections and editing versions of this manuscript. Thank you, friends.

About the Author

Kathryn Rombs received her doctorate in philosophy from Fordham University, where she specialized in the philosophy of religion and Thomas Aquinas. She has taught at various universities, most recently at the University of Dallas. She and her husband, Ron, usually raise their six kids in Irving, Texas, but they currently reside in Frascati, Italy, just outside Rome. Kathryn is the founder and president of Mighty Is Her Call, Inc., a ministry that elevates Catholic mothers and seeks to reveal the Christlike nature of the vocation of motherhood. The ministry's blog features the writing of many Catholic mothers, and the ministry's retreats are a powerful way for mothers to refocus and recharge in their profoundly important vocation. Explore the ministry's website www.mightyishercall.com and visit Kathryn's personal blog, "Eucharistic Motherhood," at www.kathrynrombs.com.